AN INTRODUCTION
TO THE LEGAL SYSTEM
OF THE UNITED STATES

by

E. ALLAN FARNSWORTH

Professor of Law
Columbia University School of Law

Corrected First Edition

Published for the

PARKER SCHOOL OF FOREIGN AND COMPARATIVE LAW
COLUMBIA UNIVERSITY IN THE CITY OF NEW YORK

by
Oceana Publications, Inc.

1975

© Copyright 1963, 1975 by E. Allan Farnsworth

Library of Congress Catalog Card No. 74-29388

ISBN 0-379-00255-8

MANUFACTURED IN THE UNITED STATES OF AMERICA

PREFACE

This corrected edition affords an opportunity for a retrospective look at the reception this book has had during its first decade. Its purpose was to fill the need of those not trained in our legal system — both foreign lawyers and American laymen — for a brief introductory text emphasizing its fundamentals. It appears to have accomplished this purpose. Because it emphasizes fundamentals rather than details, it has tended to remain current in spite of normal changes in the legal system.

Foreign lawyers have made use of it here and in their own countries. It has been used as a basic text at the Salzburg Seminar in American Studies, the Leyden-Amsterdam-Columbia Program in American Law, and the Orientation Program in American Law run by the Association of American Law Schools. It has been translated into Arabic, Korean, Portuguese, Serbo-Croatian and Vietnamese.

The book has also proved useful to American laymen. It has been assigned as a text or as supplementary reading in American Colleges, and it has been recommended for students considering the choice of a career in law.

The occasion seems an appropriate one to express the hope that this brief introduction may continue to be of help to those who would have a firmer grasp of our legal system.

E. Allan Farnsworth

New York
January 1975

TO MY

FATHER AND MOTHER

TABLE OF CONTENTS

Note on Terminology

It will be helpful, at the outset, to clear up the considerable ambiguity that surrounds the terms "law" and "common law." The word "law" in the English language is used to refer to both the sum of all legal rules (*ius, droit, diritto, derecho, Recht*) and the express rule laid down by legislative authority (*lex, loi, legge, ley, Gesetz*). Originally the term "common law" described that part of the law of England which was non-statutory and common to the whole land rather than local. It may still be used in much the same sense, as in the phrase "at common law," to refer to the law, usually of England, during the early part of its development and before widespread legislation. The American lawyer may use it in at least three other senses. First, he may use it to refer to the law which is laid down by the courts rather than by the legislatures. In this book the term "case law" is used for this purpose; "decisional law" is used to include the law as laid down by other tribunals, such as administrative tribunals, in addition to courts. "Statute law" is used to refer to the enactments of legislatures; "legislation" is used in its broadest sense to include such similar forms of law as constitutions, treaties, administrative regulations, and the like, as well as statute law. Second, he may use the term "common law" to refer to the body of rules applied by the common law courts as distinguished from the special courts of equity or admiralty. The term is not used in this sense in this book. Third, he may use it to refer to his country as a "common law" country, whose law is based on English law, as opposed to a "civil law" country, whose law is derived from the Roman law tradition. This is the sense in which these terms are used in this book. The term "civil" is also sometimes used in the United States in opposition to "criminal." It is used in this book in this sense only in such terms as "civil case" and "civil procedure." The term "civil law" is not ordinarily used in the United States to refer to the subject matter of a civil code, in opposition, for example, to "commercial law."

Part One

Sources and Techniques

Chapter I

Historical Background

*American law has two distinctive ingredients: a singular variety of
federalism and a common law tradition. How did federalism take
shape during the establishment of the union? How did the common law win acceptance during the formative era?*

ESTABLISHMENT OF THE UNION[1]

Rapid change has been the rule rather than the exception
during the course of American history. Scarcely three and a half
centuries have passed since the start of the colonial period,
which is commonly dated from the first English settlement at
Jamestown, Virginia in 1607. In less than two hundred years
since they declared their independence in 1776, the thirteen
colonies of under three million inhabitants clustered near the
Atlantic seaboard have become fifty states of one hundred and
eighty-five million inhabitants, spreading from ocean to ocean
and beyond.

Along with change there has, from the outset, been diversity—of religions, of nationalities, and of economic groups. To the
colonies came Anglicans, Baptists, Huguenots, Presbyterians,
Puritans, Quakers, and Roman Catholics. Among the English
majority were pockets of Dutch, French, Germans, Irish, Scots,
and Swedes. They lived as merchants, artisans, plantation owners, small farmers, and backwoodsmen. But most important,
there was diversity in the political organization of the colonies,
which were entirely separate units under the English crown.
Some were royal provinces ruled directly by a royal governer
appointed by the king. Others were proprietary provinces with

---

[1] Part of the material in this section is adapted from Dowling, *Cases on
Constitutional Law* 50-69 (6th ed. 1959), with permission of the publisher,
Foundation Press, Inc.

political control vested by royal grant in a proprietor or group of proprietors. Still others were corporate colonies under royal charters which generally gave them more freedom from crown control than either of the other forms. Each of the colonies had its own independent evolution and its own largely separate existence until the events which led up to the Revolution put an end to their self-sufficiency. No adequate comprehension of the American legal system is possible without an understanding of the way in which these individual colonies were welded together into a single nation under a Constitution which has, with relatively little amendment, withstood the stress of diversity and the strain of change from 1789 until today.

The events which provoked the American Revolution arose in large part out of the measures taken by Britain to solve three of her major problems of the mid-eighteenth century: first, the need for additional revenue, some of which, it was thought, the colonists should contribute; second, the demand for enforcement of commercial regulations by British merchants interested in preserving colonial markets and sources of supply; and third, the difficulty of control of new territories, involving administration, land organization, and protection against Indians. In reaction to these measures, which the colonists found oppressive of their liberties, the First Continental Congress met in Philadelphia in 1774. Composed of some fifty-five delegates from almost all the colonies, it was harbinger of union among the colonies and of war with England. The colonists were anxious to assure their enjoyment of rights which Englishmen had under case law and under the English Bill of Rights of 1689 and the other great enactments of which they felt they had been deprived. This assembly, unauthorized by the Crown, represented a great advance toward united colonial action. From this moment forward there was always in being a public body devoted to the common cause of the colonies. The forceful Declaration and Resolves issued by this First Congress set out the arguments of the colonists and demanded that Parliment cease its interference in matters of taxation and internal polity. But the Congress rejected a proposed plan of colonial union.

By 1775 when the Second Continental Congress convened, fighting between the colonists and the British had already begun. Despite its dubious status, this body assumed authority over the colonies as a whole and instigated preparations for war. In spite of the hostilities, there was reluctance to break with England,

and only after long delay were all of the colonies brought into line and independence declared in July, 1776. The Declaration of Independence detailed the colonists' grievances and epitomized much of the revolutionary theory. The preamble, which calls attention to the "station to which the Laws of Nature and of Nature's God entitle" the colonists and to the rights with which men are "endowed by the Creator" reflects the influence of theories of natural law under which the Revolution was justified. The language is, however, not that of union but only that of "free and independent states." It did not unite the colonies among themselves, but only severed their ties with England.

By 1777 a committee of the Second Continental Congress, at work on the problem of colonial union, had drafted Articles of Confederation, but these were not finally ratified until 1781. This was the first serious attempt at federal union. However, each state was jealous of its newly acquired sovereignty, conscious of its own special interests, and hopeful of its own distinctive kind of reform. The Continental Congress which was created under the Articles resembled an association of diplomatic representatives of the various states in which each state had an equal vote. There was no provision for a separate national executive or judiciary. The most conspicuous reason for the ultimate failure of the Confederation was the lack of powers granted to Congress. It had no authority to levy taxes, to regulate interstate or foreign commerce, or to ensure state compliance with treaties. It was against this background that many of the best minds in America came to the Constitutional Convention in Philadelphia in May, 1787, to try to preserve the union.

Certainly they approached their task equipped with many of the governmental theories of their day, but what is most impressive is the degree of realism which characterized their deliberations. Beginning in 1776 state constitutions had been adopted, occasionally amid bitter political rivalries. A number of the delegates had participated in the drafting of these documents and had been members of the Continental Congress. It was in large measure experience on which they relied—experience under colonial rule, under state constitutions, and under the Articles of Confederation. The chief problem before them was to form a strong union without obliterating the states as constituent, in some respects autonomous, parts of the system; it was through the states that experience gained in the colonial period was to be preserved. Widely differing points of view were ably represented among the delegates and the result was, of course, a compromise. As the Convention progressed the movement away from a loose league of sovereign states, as the Confederation had been, grew more pronounced. Instead of adding coercive and other powers to patch up the old league, the delegates ultimately arrived at the crucial decision of the Convention, to have a central government with widened powers designed to operate on individulas rather than states.

In September, 1787, the Constitution was signed and submitted to Congress, to become effective upon its acceptance by two thirds of the states. This occurred in July, 1788, and the first President, George Washington, was inaugurated in April, 1789. The final text of the Constitution shows the influence of principles developed in the course of history. The notions that the people are sovereign and that their government is based on a social compact may be found in the preamble, in the provisions for state conventions to ratify the completed Constitution, and in the idea that powers are "granted" to the central government. The theory that the federal government is one of limited powers is evidenced by their enumeration, including the power to tax, to wage war, to regulate interstate and foreign commerce, and to make treaties; as to the residue each of the states has the capacity to make law. The concept of the separation of the federal legislative, executive, and judicial powers is implied by the form of the Constitution, with three separate major articles each of which delineates one of these three major, and presumably distinct, powers. And the belief that constitutional rights should be embodied in a written instrument is evident from the document itself. The Constitution contained no guarantees of basic human rights. But in 1789 Congress promptly proposed the first ten amendments to the Constitution, which are popularly known as the Bill of Rights because many of them are concerned with the rights of the individual against the federal government. They were finally ratified in 1791.

One of the tenets of the framers of the Constitution was that the interpretation of constitutional rights should be entrusted to specialists. The judiciary article provides for an independent judicial power operating, like the legislative and executive, upon both states and individuals, and vests this power in a Supreme Court and in such inferior courts as Congress "may from time to time ordain and establish." Their jurisdiction expressly includes cases arising under the Constitution and coupled with this is a statement that the "Constitution, and the Laws of the United States which shall be made in Pursuance thereof, and all Treaties made, or which shall be made, under the Authority of the United States, shall be the supreme Law of the Land." But there is no specific provision giving the federal courts the power of judicial review[2] over either federal or state legislation, although many of the delegates must have assumed it would have that power.

In 1789 Congress passed the First Judiciary Act which, on its face, contemplated federal judicial review of state court decisions in certain cases. The Act implemented the judiciary article of the Constitution by creating lower federal courts and by defining their jurisdiction along with that of the Supreme Court. The state courts had already exercised judicial review over state legislation under state constitutions and continued to do so, and the newly created lower federal courts began to strike down state legislation as contrary to the federal Constitution itself. Judicial review was natural because of colonial experience with review of legislation and because federal and state constitutions had come to embody notions of limitations on government. Since the federal government was a government of limited powers only, those granted to it by the Constitution, it could be inferred that the federal judiciary was also to determine whether Congress had exceeded these powers. This inference was borne out by the opinion of Chief Justice John Marshall[3] in the landmark case of *Marbury* v. *Madison*,[4] decided in 1803. In that case the Supreme Court refused to give effect to a section of a federal statute, on the ground that Congress in enacting it had exceeded the powers granted it by the Constitution, and thereby firmly established that federal legislation was subject to judicial review in the federal courts. A few years later it affirmed its authority under the federal Constitution to pass upon the validity

---

2 Judicial review, as that term is used in American constitutional law, refers to the power of a court to pass upon the constitutionality of legislation and to refuse to give effect to legislation which it decides to be invalid on constitutional grounds.

3 John Marshall (1755-1835) was the fourth Chief Justice of the United States, from 1801 until 1835. He had previously served in a number of public offices, including that of Secretary of State. His only formal education consisted of two months of law lectures at the College of William and Mary. He was the author of many of the most significant opinions of that court during this crucial period and is generally regarded as its greatest Chief Justice.

4 5 U.S. (1 Cranch) 137 (1803).

of state statutes,[5] an authority which has been one of the great unifying forces in the United States. Justice Holmes[6] of the Supreme Court of the United States has observed, "I do not think the United States would come to an end if we lost our power to declare an Act of Congress void. I do think the Union would be imperiled if we could not make that declaration as to the laws of the several states."[7] A state court, too, may refuse to enforce a state or federal statute on the ground that it violates the federal Constitution, but this determination is subject to review by the Supreme Court of the United States.[8] The subject of judicial review is discussed in more detail in later chapters, as is the hierarchy of such authorities as constitutions, treaties, statutes, and judicial decisions, among the various sources of law in the newly formed union. For present purposes it is sufficient to note that in spite of the surrender by the states of some of their sovereignty when they joined the union, each state was left to work out its own law as best it might, subject only to the restraints imposed under the Constitution.

Origins of American Law

Just as there was no uniform evolution of political organization in the colonies, there was no uniform growth of colonial law. The same diversity as to extent of crown control, date of settlement, and conditions of development resulted in thirteen separate legal systems, each with its distinct historical background. Furthermore, as the boundaries of the United States were extended, large areas were added which had been subject to Spanish, Mexican, or French sovereignty for substantial periods of time. A few states, most notably Louisiana, still show the imprint of such origins, and the civil law institution of com-

---

[5] *Fletcher* v. *Peck*, 10 U.S. (6 Cranch) 87 (1810).

[6] Oliver Wendell Holmes (1841-1935), a graduate of Harvard College and the Harvard Law School, practiced law in Boston, served briefly as professor of law at Harvard, and then for twenty years as judge and later chief justice of the Supreme Judicial Court of Massachusetts. In 1902 he was appointed an associate justice of the United States Supreme Court, where the quality of his dissenting opinions won him the title of the "Great Dissenter." He resigned because of ill health in 1932. His most famous work is *The Common Law* (1881), based on a series of lectures.

[7] Holmes, *Collected Legal Papers* 295-96 (1920). In Corwin (ed.), *The Constitution of the United States: Analysis and Interpretation* 1241 (1953) there is a list of only seventy-three acts of Congress held unconstitutional in whole or in part by the Supreme Court from its inception to June 30, 1952.

[8] See p. 41 *infra*.

munity property can be found in eight states today. Nevertheless, the similarities among state law far outweigh the differences and there is on the whole an unmistakable family resemblance to the law of England. That the influence should have been English is hardly surprising in view of the language and nationality of most of the colonists; that this influence should have met with the resistance which it did calls for some explanation.

There were at least three impediments to the immediate acceptance of English law in the early colonial period. The first was the dissatisfaction with some aspects of English justice on the part of many of the colonists, who had migrated to the New World in order to escape from what they regarded as intolerable conditions in the mother country. This was particularly true for those who had come in search of religious, political, or economic freedom. A second and more significant impediment was the lack of trained lawyers, which continued to retard the development of American law throughout the seventeenth century. The rigorous life in the colonies had little attraction for English lawyers. English law books were not readily available, and few among the early settlers had any legal training. The third impediment was the disparity of the conditions in the two lands. Particularly in the beginning, life was more primitive in the colonies and familiar English institutions which were copied were often rough copies at best. The early settlers did not carry English law in its entirety with them when they came, and the process by which it was absorbed in the face of these impediments was not a simple one.

The extent to which English case law, as distinguished from statute law, was in effect, either in theory or in practice, during the early history of the colonies is not free from dispute. It is clear that although the British Parliament had legislative power over the colonies, it was not fully exercised. Although acts passed prior to the initial settlement of a colony, if adapted to the circumstances, were generally regarded as being in force in that colony as well as in England, acts passed after initial settlement did not extend to the colonies unless expressly provided. Power to legislate had been conferred upon the colonies themselves, and each had its own legislature with at least one elective branch and with considerable control over internal affairs. Codification was common in the early stages of some of the colonies partly because of the absence of law books and the lack of a trained bar, and partly because of colonial notions of law reform. Colonial legislation was reviewed by administrative authorities in the mother country and might be set aside if it was "contrary" or "repugnant" to the laws or commercial policy of England. Colonial legislation was also subject to judicial review and might be held to be void when appeals from judgments of colonial courts were taken to England. But no systematic control was exercised until the end of the seventeenth century.

During the seventeenth century the justice which was administered was often lacking in technicalities and was sometimes based on a general sense of right as derived from the Bible and the law of nature. Court procedure, at least outside of the superior courts, was tailored to suit American needs and was marked by an informality of proceedings and a simplicity of pleadings befitting a less technical system in which the judges were, for the most part, untutored in the law. The model may have been the local courts in England which would have been familiar to many of the colonists. Substantive law, as well as procedure, began to respond to colonial needs. In England the feudal policy in favor of keeping estates in land intact had resulted in the rule of primogeniture, the exclusive right of the eldest son to inherit the land of the father.[9] In America, however, the demand for equality and for a more just distribution of improved land eventually caused the abandonment of this rule in favor of distribution among all children, subject to varying rights of a surviving spouse. This practice began as custom in the northern colonies. It was confirmed there by legislation and, in spite of a notable case in which Connecticut's statute was held void on review in England as contrary to English law,[10] it had spread southward by legislation to all of the states by the end of the eighteenth century.

The beginning of the eighteenth century saw considerable refinement of colonial law and a concurrent increase in the influence of English case law. Review of colonial legislation had become more thorough. With the growth of trade and the increase in population—to some three hundred thousand in 1700 —the ranks of trained lawyers were swelled and the courts of review began to be manned by professionals. Some were English

---

[9] The rule of primogeniture was not changed in England until the Administration of Estates Act in 1926.

[10] *Winthrop* v. *Lechmere* (1728). This case is discussed in Smith, *Appeals to the Privy Council from the American Plantations* 537 (1950).

lawyers who had immigrated, while others were native lawyers who had studied in London or as apprentices in law offices in the colonies. English law books had become increasingly available and it has been said that by the time of the Revolution William Blackstone's[11] widely read *Commentaries on the Laws of England,* which first appeared between 1765 and 1769, had sold nearly as many copies in America as in England. Interest in English law was stimulated by the necessity of dealing in commercial matters with Englishmen trained in its ways and by the desirability of reliance upon its principles to support the colonists' grievances against the Crown. By the time of the Revolution English law had come to be generally well regarded and each colony had a bar of trained, able, and respected professionals, capable of working with a refined and technical system. The colonial legal profession, especially in the cities, had achieved both social standing and economic success. It was also politically active: twenty-five of the fifty-six signers of the Declaration of Independence were lawyers.

It is therefore not surprising that most of the thirteen original states formally "received", that is adopted, by constitution or statute, some part of the law of England along with their own colonial enactments. The formulas varied, but a typical reception provision might include that part of English law which "together did form the law of said colony" prior to such a specific date as 1607 or 1776. In other states the reception of English law was achieved by judicial decision alone. As additional states were carved out of the western territories similar procedures were followed with regard to reception. While the details of the reception of English law differ considerably from state to state, it is clear that the changes and developments in English law after the date of reception for a particular state have no binding force at all in that state.

The Revolution resulted in a setback to the influence of English law in some of the new states because of political antipathy. In a few, anti-British sentiment was implemented by statutes prohibiting the citation of English decisions handed

---

11 William Blackstone (1723-1780), an English barrister, began the first university lectures on the common law in England at Oxford in 1753. In 1758 he was appointed to the first professorship of English law at that university. He is remembered chiefly for his *Commentaries,* which went through eight editions in his lifetime.

down after independence.[12] At the same time the quality of the practicing bar as a whole was impaired. Some, who had been loyalists, had left the country before the end of the war; others, seizing the opportunity for leadership, accepted political or judicial posts under the new government. The standards and repute of the remainder deteriorated in many communities. The era of the lay judge was not entirely over and during the early nineteenth century the state of Rhode Island had a farmer as chief justice and a blacksmith as a member of its highest court. There was not even an adequate body of American case law which could be used by those judges who had the ability and inclination to do so. Although reports of cases began to be published at the end of the eighteenth century, they were few in number. The opportunity for broadening the base of American law was considerable. There was some inclination to look to French and Roman law, and European writers were cited, particularly in the fields of commercial law and conflict of laws where English treatises were inadequate. But few judges were versed in modern foreign languages and, while English treatises and reports were available the *Code Napoléon* did not appear until after the beginning of the nineteenth century. Blackstone's *Commentaries,* which had been published in an American edition in 1803, were particularly influential.

During the first part of the nineteenth century agriculture and trade dominated the economy as energies went into the westward expansion and the production of staples for European markets. Judges labored to shape English legal materials to fit the conditions of their particular jurisdictions. They examined the pre-Revolutionary English law to determine its applicability to American conditions and laid the foundations of such fields as contracts, torts, sale of goods, real property, and conflict of laws. There was constant legislative intervention in such areas as procedure, criminal law, marriage and divorce, descent and distribution, wills and administration. Sometimes the law grew out of local usages or needs. The customs of western farmers and gold miners formed the basis for water and mining law in some of the western states. Some of the prairie states where cattle-raising was the means of livelihood and wood for fences was scarce, changed the English rule that the owner of

---

[12] A common toast of the time is said to have been: "The Common Law of England: may wholesome statutes soon root out this engine of oppression from America." Warren, *A History of the American Bar* 227 (1913).

cattle is liable without fault for damage which they may cause to a neighboring crop-owner. But it was also an era of great "national" treatises such as James Kent's[13] *Commentaries on American Law,* published from 1826 to 1830, and nine works by Joseph Story[14] published from 1832 to 1845. These treatises, which went through many revisions, played an important role in promoting uniformity by helping to counter the forces which contributed to diversity.

Out of the first half of the century came a set of institutions and procedures which still survive. But the functions which they now perform and the issues with which they now deal often differ from those of the earlier formative period. The years of the Civil War, 1861 to 1865, mark a rough but convenient division between this period and the later development of American law. The years after the war saw a rapid increase in population and its concentration in the cities. They witnessed the growth of large scale industry, transportation, and communication, with attendant complexities in the corporate form of organization. From 1850 to 1860 the population of the state of Minnesota increased from 6,000 to 172,000. In 1790 only about three percent of the people in the United States lived in the six cities which had 8,000 or more inhabitants; by 1890 about one out of three Americans lived in a city of 4,000 or more. From 1869 to 1900 railway mileage grew from 30,000 to 166,000 miles. In 1876 the first telephone message was sent and in 1882 Edison's electric power plant began operation in New York City.

In this rapidly expanding industrial society the creation of a stable system of law took on increased importance. Development continued in such fields as corporations, public service companies, railroads, and insurance. But during the final quarter of the century much of the law of the formative era began to crystallize and the role of the judge became one of systematiz-

---

13 James Kent (1763-1847) became the first professor of law at Columbia College in 1793. He resigned in 1798 to go on the New York Supreme Court and was appointed Chancellor of the state in 1814. Upon his retirement in 1823 he returned to Columbia, and during this period he published his *Commentaries on American Law,* a collection of his lectures dealing with nearly all phases of contemporary substantive law.

14 Joseph Story (1779-1845) was appointed to the United States Supreme Court in 1811. In 1829, while retaining his seat on the Court, he became a professor of law at the Harvard Law School, where he reorganized the curriculum and revitalized the school. His nine commentaries developed from his lectures on subjects ranging from the Constitution to conflict of laws.

ing rather than of creating. As the volume of case law increased, the uncertainty which had been inevitable in earlier years became unpopular and efforts turned toward a search for predictability. The principal achievements of the courts were the ordering of the system and the logical development of details. It is significant that the treatises of this period were more specialized than those of the first half of the century. Some creative activity was to be found in the legislatures, which had been more active in reform than the judiciary until the Civil War, but popular esteem for the courts was at its height and aggressive judges asserted their judicial authority in holding legislation to constitutional standards.

By the turn of the century, however, the methodical accretion of rules, case by case, had begun to lose some of its popular appeal. The watchword of the courts was still stability, but they had failed to keep pace with the demands of the rapidly changing political and economic order. The shape of things to come might have been foretold from the organization in 1886 of the American Federation of Labor, the first of the great national labor unions, from the creation in 1887 of the Interstate Commerce Commission, the first of the great national regulatory agencies, and from the enactment in 1890 of the Sherman Act, the first of the great federal antitrust statutes.   And so the present century ushered in a new era of change and creativity in law, marked by an increased pace of legislation, particularly social legislation, and by greater reliance upon administrative agencies instead of courts. During the second decade most of the state workmen's compensation laws were enacted. At about the same time modern administrative power began to take its present shape, both in the nation and in the states. Some of these more recent developments will be dealt with later.

The influence of English law in America, which had virtually ended by the time of the Civil War, is negligible today. Only infrequently are the more recent English cases cited in contemporary American judicial opinions and even more rarely will a question arise which turns on the reception of English law. Yet the fundamental approach, much of the vocabulary, and many of the principles and concepts of the common law are as familiar in the United States as in England. English cases, although in relatively small numbers, are still part of the "taught tradition" in American law schools. And while American lawyers and judges may commonly ignore English authorities, they are, nevertheless, conditioned by English ideas which were imported into American law over a century and a half ago. Foremost among these are: first, the concept of supremacy of law, as exemplified in this country by the distinctive principle that even the state is subject to judicial review under constitutional standards; second, the tradition of precedent, according to which later decisions are based on earlier cases; and third, the notion of a trial as a contentious proceeding, a contest, often before a jury, in which the adversary parties take the initiative and in which the role of the judge is that of umpire rather than inquisitor. These will be explored in later chapters.

SUGGESTED READINGS

There is no completely satisfactory comprehensive history of American law from early colonial times until today. Hurst, *The Growth of American Law: The Law Makers* (1950) traces its development from 1790 to 1940 in terms of the men who made it. A well-documented discussion of the early sources, with emphasis on land law, can be found in Chapter 4 of Powell, *The Law of Real Property* (1949). Aumann, *The Changing American Legal System: Some Selected Phases* (1940) emphasizes the development up to the Civil War, as does Pound, *The Formative Era of American Law* (1938), a series of four lectures.

Chapter II

Legal Education

In spite of their diversity, American law schools share two characteristics: their graduate level and their professional objective. Why is this the form of legal education and how does the case method of instruction serve its ends?

DIVERSITY

The development of the American legal system has been influenced by the kind of education that lawyers have received, and legal education in turn reflects the diversity of that legal system. The study of law for more than forty thousand law students today means study in one of some one hundred and sixty law schools, and nearly all lawyers now being admitted to practice hold degrees from these schools. But because the number of institutions is large and because there is no federal control of education, the diversity among these institutions is much greater than in countries where the number of law faculties is smaller or where there is some regulation by the national government. Most law schools have been approved by the American Bar Association, and two thirds of them have met the somewhat stricter standards for membership in the Association of American Law Schools. This discussion will be confined to these member schools, almost all of which are part of a university. The university may be private, with no state connection, as are Columbia, Harvard, and Yale, or it may be supported by one of the fifty states. The school may be regarded as a "local" law school in the sense that its students come from and intend to practice in the region where it is located and there is a tendency to emphasize local law on problems of particular significance to the area, or it may be one of the "national" law schools which, like the three just mentioned, attempts to prepare its graduates more generally for practice in any state.[1] It may have only a full-time program of study lasting for three years, or it may also have a part-time program, usually of evening study, requiring a longer time. It may be one of the few law schools with more than one thousand students, or one of the handful with less than one hundred.[2] Yet in spite of the great variety in American law schools, there are several characteristics which they have in common and which distinguish them from their sister institutions in most of the rest of the world. The most striking of these are their graduate level and professional objective and the case method of instruction, each of which had its origin in the development of legal education during the nineteenth century.

Graduate Level and Professional Objective

It may seem surprising that legal education should be thought of as being on the university graduate level in a country where an established tradition of university education for the practice of law is not more than a century old. After the Revolution legal education deteriorated along with the bar. Until well past the middle of the nineteenth century it was principally in the hands of the practitioners, as at the Inns of Court in England, and the accepted way of preparing for the bar was by "reading law." This usually meant a more or less desultory apprenticeship consisting largely of the performance of routine tasks in the office of a practicing lawyer, together with the reading of the American edition of Blackstone's *Commentaries* and later of Kent's *Commentaries*.[3] There were some exceptions. In 1753 at Oxford University, William Blackstone had begun the first university lectures on the common law in England, and before the turn of the century a small number of American universities had followed this example. A chair of law was established at William and Mary College in 1779; James Kent became professor of law at Columbia College in 1793; and there were a

---

1 See Jones, *Local Law Schools* vs. *National Law Schools: A Comparison of Concepts, Functions and Opportunities,* 10 J. Legal Ed. 281 (1958).

2 Even among the three schools named above, the enrollments vary from over 1600 for Harvard to under 900 for Columbia and under 600 for Yale. Tuition and fees range from less than $200 a year to more than $1500 a year, but may in case of need be more than offset by scholarship or loan aid.

3 Many men, including President Abraham Lincoln, prepared for the bar largely by self-directed reading of such works.

few others. In addition, independent schools of law, in which a lawyer undertook to instruct more students than he could accommodate in his office, grew up outside the universities as offshoots of the apprenticeship system. The most notable of these was the Litchfield Law School which lasted from 1784 to 1833.

However the present-day American law school did not begin to take shape until Justice Joseph Story reorganized the Harvard Law School in 1829, twelve years after its establishment. It is to Story that the dominantly professional orientation of the American law school is largely due. The occupants of the early university chairs of law had, like Blackstone, regarded law as a part of liberal education. But under Story, legal and liberal education were divorced and law was taught on the assumption that the student had acquired a sufficient background in the liberal arts before he was admitted to law school. The idea took hold and the number of such university law schools with one or two year courses had increased to thirty-one by 1870. However, these schools had no academic admissions requirements and no attempt was made to ensure that the students had the background of liberal education that Story had assumed. Most had faculties of from one to three professors. The first half of the century had been a period of rampant Jacksonian democracy[4] marked by the exaltation of the common man and carrying with it the implication that a man had an almost inherent right to practice law.[5] The legal profession in the United States has never been the province of a select elite, and egalitarian feeling ran especially high at this time. Even the general requirements of preparatory study or apprenticeship for admission to the bar which had existed in the early 1800's had been abandoned. The new law schools, in spite of their university connections, were vocational and lacking in distinction.

Beginning in about 1870, the expansion and industrialization following the Civil War gave new vitality to the training of the lawyers who were to practice the more complex law of this era. The American Bar Association was formed in 1878 and its section on legal education evidenced the interest of the

---

[4] "Jacksonian democracy" took its name from Andrew Jackson, who was President from 1828 to 1836, and had as a premise that the popular mandate is the ultimate sanction of all governmental activity.

[5] From 1851 to 1933 the Constitution of the State of Indiana provided that "Every person of good moral character, being a voter, shall be entitled to admission to practice law in all courts of justice."

organized bar in this field. From this group, the Association of American Law Schools was organized in 1900 for the improvement of legal education. By 1905 it was able to require of its members the present minimum of three years of law study. By 1923 it had established one, by 1925 two, and by 1952 three years of college education as a prerequisite for admission to law school, and many students today have completed the four years necessary for the college bachelor's degree.[6] However, no specific college courses are ordinarily required for admission. It is anomalous that in spite of the graduate character which legal education has assumed, the degree offered at most schools remains the bachelor of laws (LL.B.)[7] and not a doctorate. While some institutions offer additional work leading to the degree of master of laws (LL.M) and doctor of the science of law (J.S.D. or S.J.D.), these are rarely taken as preparation for the practice of law.[8]

The requirement of a college education as a prerequisite to the study of law coupled with the disappearance some fifty years earlier of any requirement of an office apprenticeship has made it even easier to justify the professional emphasis of the training. Nevertheless, beginning in the 1920's there has been some broadening of the curriculum to include non-legal materials, particularly from the social sciences. A landmark study was conducted by the Columbia School of Law in 1926 to 1928, and most schools make periodic, if less extensive, reexaminations of their curricula. Yet in spite of recent trends, legal education in the United States is still intensely professional when compared with university education in law in most other countries of the world.

So it is that an American law student usually does not enter

---

[6] The American student usually graduates from high school, the end of the free public school system, at the age of 17 or 18. He may then seek admission to a state or private college or university where he will receive a general college education leading to a bachelor's degree at the end of four years, by the age of 21 or 22. An institution which includes several faculties, e. g., an undergraduate faculty, graduate faculty, and professional schools, is usually called a "university"; while one with only an undergraduate faculty is ordinarily called a "college." A bachelor's degree is commonly required for the study of medicine, which is itself a four year course.

[7] Some law schools award the degree of doctor of laws (J.D.) to some or all of their graduates instead of the traditional LL.B. This should not be confused with the degree of doctor of laws (LL.D.) that is awarded as an honorary rather than an earned degree.

[8] Candidates for the J.S.D. or S.J.D. degree usually intend to teach law.

law school until the age of twenty-one or twenty-two, after at least three years of college and frequently after graduation. The leading schools have several times more applications than they have vacancies and the successful applicant is chosen on the basis of his college record and often a nation-wide examination now used by about half of the law schools to test aptitude for law study. Where selection is careful, fewer than one in ten of his fellows will be lost because of academic failure; where it is not, the rate of failure is much higher. He is almost certainly interested in some form of law practice since this kind of highly professional, demanding, and costly graduate training is not often pursued in preparation for a non-legal career in business or government. His three years of study are devoted to such technical subjects as contracts, torts, real and personal property, trusts, evidence, procedure, equity, criminal law, commercial law, bankruptcy, corporation law, taxation, trade regulation, constitutional law, administrative law, labor law, family law, agency, partnership, and conflict of laws,[9] together with a few broader offerings such as jurisprudence, comparative law, and legal history, but to the exclusion of economics, sociology, political science or government, which he is assumed to have mastered in his earlier education. Anywhere from less than one third to well over two thirds of his program will be prescribed for him, and the rest will be elective. During this three year period of intensive professional training, the student is subjected to that peculiarly American method of instruction known as the case method.

Case Method

The introduction of the case method came with the publication in 1871 by Professor Christopher Columbus Langdell[10] of the Harvard Law School of his casebook on contracts, an ordered collection of cases—appellate court opinions—for the use of his students. He had concluded that the shortest and best way of mastering the few basic principles on which he thought the law to be based was by studying the opinions in which they were embodied. He also believed that the instruction should be

---

9 These fields are described in Part Two *infra*.

10 Christopher Columbus Langdell (1826-1896) was a New York lawyer who became professor of law at Harvard Law School in 1870. His principal achievement as professor and later dean was the introduction of the case method of instruction.

of such a character that the pupils "might at least derive a greater advantage from attending it than from devoting the time to private study." Once law professors began to put collections of cases in the hands of their students, the next step was to abandon the traditional lecture method and to pose questions and discuss with the students the cases which they were to have read before class—the so-called Socratic method. Because the cases came from many jurisdictions they were not always consistent and the method took on a comparative aspect in which the student was required to evaluate conflicting rules in the context of an actual situation. By the end of the first decade of this century these techniques had been generally accepted in law schools throughout the country. But if Langdell thought that all the law could be learned from cases, he was mistaken. Not only is much of American law found elsewhere than in cases, but the method is inordinately time consuming if the objective is to learn all or even a substantial part of the law. In recent times the case method has been justified on the ground that by requiring the student to state, analyze, evaluate, and compare concrete fact situations, to use sources as they are used by lawyers and judges, and then to formulate his own basic propositions, it serves to train him in the skills and techniques of the profession and to develop his powers of analysis, reason, and expression, goals which are placed above the encyclopedic knowledge of legal rules.[11] The cases are often supplemented or replaced by problems which may call for counselling and which are equally effective in courses where the sources are largely statutory. The case method is ideally suited to the peculiarly professional character of legal education in the United States but it must be conceded that it has helped to isolate law from other branches of learning. An increasing awareness of this difficulty, of the limitations of appellate court opinions, and of a slackening of student interest, has led to some diminution in the stress on cases. But the emphasis is still on development of the student's critical

---

[11] See Morgan, *The Case Method*, 4 J. Legal Ed. 379 (1952); Patterson, *The Case Method in American Legal Education: Its Origins and Objectives*, 4 J. Legal Ed. 1 (1951). The case method is reflected in the typical law school examination question, which poses an unfamiliar hypothetical fact situation, often a borderline case, and may ask the student to decide the case and present supporting reasons or perhaps to argue the case for one side or to advise a client. Emphasis is on analysis and reasoning rather than on a "correct" conclusion. Law school examinations are written.

faculties by requiring him to prepare in advance of class and to exercise his independent judgment.

So it is that the American law student still finds the case method the basic pattern in most of his classes, even when they number over a hundred students,[12] and is expected to spend two hours reading his casebooks in preparation for each of his twelve to fifteen hours of class per week. But the casebooks which once contained only cases now contain text, problems, statutes, legal forms, and even materials from related disciplines, and a number of other activities are available to enrich the student's educational experience. In seminars, limited to a small number of students, he may benefit from more informal discussion and get practice in research and writing.[13] In moot court he may participate as counsel, usually on appeal, in a simulated case before judges drawn from the faculty, the bar, the judiciary, and the student body. Or he may receive practical experience during the academic year under a cooperative arrangement which his school may have with the local legal aid bureau where students participate in giving legal assistance to the poor. And if he is fortunate enough to rank near the top of his class he will be invited to compete for the honor of working on his school's law review, and may help to write and edit one of the nearly one hundred such journals, which include America's most distinguished legal periodicals and which are traditionally edited by students.[14] From this kind of training come the candidates for admission to the bar.

SUGGESTED READINGS

The standard study on legal education is Harno, *Legal Education in the United States* (1953). Current thinking in the field can be found in the *Journal of Legal Education,* the quarterly periodical of the Association of American Law Schools published since 1948. One example is Currie, *The Materials of Law Study,* 3 J. Legal Ed. 331 (1951), 8 J. Legal Ed. 1 (1955), a history of legal education with emphasis on developments in this century. The subject is also discussed in Chapter 6 of Blau-

---

[12] In the larger schools classes are usually taught in sections so as not to exceed one hundred or one hundred and fifty students.

[13] Law students are required to make extensive use of the library for research. Harvard has over 1,000,000 volumes in its law library; Yale and Columbia have over 400,000; and Michigan has over 300,000.

[14] Law reviews are discussed at p. 83 *infra.*

stein and Porter, *The American Lawyer* (1954), a summary of a survey of the legal profession, and in Hurst, *The Growth of American Law: The Law Makers*, pp. 256-76 (1950), a history of law including legal education.

Chapter III

Legal Profession

The American lawyer is fortunate in the wide range of activities in which he may engage and in the ease with which he may move from one branch of the profession to another. Who are American lawyers, what functions do they perform, how are they organized, and what have been their contributions to the profession?

THE BAR

The regulation of the legal profession is the concern of the states, each of which has its own requirements for admission to practice. Most require two years of college and a law degree. The alternative of law office study in place of law school study still exists in some states but is rarely chosen. A few require an office apprenticeship, usually for half a year, in addition to a law degree. Each administers its own two or three day written examination, emphasizing its own law. The quality and uniformity of these examinations have been improved through the efforts of the National Conference of Bar Examiners which was organized in 1931. While only about half of all applicants succeed on the first try, many others pass on a later attempt. In all, some ten thousand persons succeed in passing these examinations each year and, after an inquiry into their character, are admitted to the bar[1] in their respective states. A lawyer's practice is usually confined to his own community for, although he may travel to represent his clients, he is only permitted to practice in a state where he has been admitted. It is customary to retain local counsel for matters in other jurisdictions. However, the lawyer

---

[1] Originally the "bar" was a partition in the courtroom separating the general public from the judges, lawyers, and others involved in the proceeding. It is now used to refer generally to the legal profession.

who moves to another state can usually be admitted without examination if he has practiced in a state where he has been admitted for a period of usually three or five years. The rules for admission to practice before the federal courts vary with the court, but generally those entitled to practice before the highest court of a state may be admitted before the federal courts upon compliance with minor formalities.

After admission, the lawyer may deal directly with clients and is free to take or reject any case which is tendered to him. He may not only practice law, but is permitted to engage in any activity which is open to other citizens. It is not uncommon for the practicing lawyer to serve on boards of directors of his corporate clients, to engage in business, and to participate actively in public affairs.[2] He remains a member of the bar even when he becomes a judge, an employee of the government or of a private business concern, or a law teacher, and he may return to private practice from these other activities. A relatively small number of lawyers give up practice for responsible executive

---

[2] The variety of public service in which the practicing lawyer may engage without leaving his practice is suggested by the careers of two contemporary leaders of the bar, Whitney North Seymour and Harrison Tweed.

Whitney North Seymour was born in 1901, graduated from the University of Wisconsin, and received his law degree from the Columbia University School of Law. He was admitted to practice in New York in 1924, and joined the firm of Simpson, Thatcher and Bartlett, becoming a partner in 1929. He has been president of the American Bar Association, president of the American Bar Foundation, president of the Association of the Bar of the City of New York, president of the Legal Aid Society of New York, president of the New York Joint Conference on Legal Education, chairman of the Carnegie Endowment for International Peace, and chairman of the Lawyers Committee for the Court of Military Appeals. He has served as Assistant Solicitor General of the United States, as a special assistant to the Attorney General during an investigation of New York waterfront activities, as a member of the New York Temporary Commission on the Courts, as a member of the Attorney General's National Committee to Study the Antitrust Laws, and as trustee of the Practising Law Institute. He has been a part-time lecturer at New York and Yale Universities.

Harrison Tweed was born in 1885, graduated from Harvard College and received his law degree from the Harvard Law School. He began practice in New York City in 1910 and in 1921 became a partner in a firm which is now known as Milbank, Tweed, Hadley and McCloy. He has served as president of the Association of the Bar of the City of New York, as president of the American Law Institute, as chairman of the New York Temporary Commission on the Courts, as chairman of the Joint Committee on Continuing Legal Education of the American Law Institute and the American Bar Association, as president and director of the Legal Aid Society of New York, as president and director of the National Legal Aid and Defender Association, as member of the Board of Overseers of Harvard College and president of the Harvard Alumni Association, as trustee of The Cooper Union, and as chairman of the board and as president of Sarah Lawrence College.

positions in commerce and industry. The mobility as well as the sense of public responsibility in the profession is evidenced by the career of Harlan Fiske Stone[3] who was, at various times, a successful New York lawyer, a professor and dean of the Columbia School of Law, Attorney General of the United States, and Chief Justice of the United States.

There is no formal division among lawyers according to function.[4] The distinction between barristers and solicitors found in England did not take root in the United Stated and there is no branch of the profession which has a special or exclusive right to appear in court, nor is there a branch which specializes in the preparation of legal instruments.[5] The American lawyer's domain includes advocacy, counselling, and drafting. Furthermore, within the sphere broadly defined as the "practice of law" the domain is exclusively his and is not open to others. In the field of advocacy, the rules are fairly clear: any individual may represent himself in court but, with the exception of a few inferior courts, only a lawyer may represent another in court. Layman are, however, authorized to represent others in formal proceedings of a judicial nature before some administrative agencies. The lines of demarcation are less clear in the areas of counselling and drafting of legal instruments, as for example between the practice of law and that of accounting in the field of federal income taxation. However, the strict approach of most American courts is indicated by a decision of New York's highest court[6] that a lawyer admitted to practice in a foreign country but not in New York is prohibited from giving legal advice to clients in New York, even though the advice is limited to the law of the foreign

---

[3] Harlan Fiske Stone (1872-1946) combined teaching and the practice of law for a time after his graduation from Amherst College and the Columbia School of Law. He served as dean of the law school at Columbia from 1910 to 1923. In 1924 he was appointed Attorney General. In 1925 he was appointed to the Supreme Court and in 1941 he succeeded Charles Evans Hughes as Chief Justice.

[4] Where the terms "attorney," "attorney-at-law," "counsellor," and "counsellor-at-law" are used it is generally for their elegance rather than for any difference in meaning.

[5] The office of notary or notary public is a minor state office with power to perform such routine functions as the attestation of writings and the administration of oaths. It requires no legal training, is often held as a part-time post by a clerk or secretary, and cannot be compared with professions bearing similar names in other legal systems.

[6] *Matter of New York County Lawyers Association* (*Roel*), 3 N.Y. 2d 224, 144 N.E. 2d 24 (1957), appeal dismissed, 355 U.S. 604 (1958) (advice on Mexican divorce law).

country where he is admitted. The foreign lawyer may, of course, advise a New York lawyer as a consultant on foreign law.

Because of the wide range of activities open to lawyers in the United States, the number of persons admitted to practice is large, well over a quarter of a million. Their income is good, although they are seldom rich and the average lawyer earns considerably less than the average doctor. Nevertheless, the young law graduate who enters the employ of a law firm, a corporation, or the government can immediately support a family. Lawyers are concentrated in the metropolitan areas with more than half in cities of over two hundred thousand, and one out of eight in New York City alone. Out of every twenty, approximately fifteen are in private practice, two are employed by private business concerns, two are in government service, and one is a member of the judiciary or the teaching profession. The one in forty who is a woman still finds her sex a hindrance in the profession.

LAWYERS IN PRIVATE PRACTICE

Among these fifteen lawyers in private practice, nine, a clear majority, are single practitioners.The remaining six practice in law firms, which are generally organized as partnerships. Four or five of these six are partners and the others are associates, a term applied to salaried lawyers employed by a firm or another lawyer. This trend toward group practice is of relatively recent origin. Throughout most of the nineteenth century law practice was general rather than specialized, its chief ingredient was advocacy rather than counselling and drafting, and the prototype of the American lawyer was the single practitioner. Marked specialization began in the latter part of that century in the large cities near the financial centers. With the growth of big business, big government, and big labor, the work of the lawyer accommodated itself to the needs of his clients for expert counselling and drafting to prevent as well as to settle disputes. The best men were attracted to this work and leadership of the bar gravitated to lawyers who rarely if ever appeared in court and who were sought after as advisors, planners, and negotiators. Today the lawyer regards it as sound practice to be continuously familiar with his clients' business problems and to participate at all steps in the shaping of their policies. Major business transactions are rarely undertaken without advice of counsel.

The breadth of vision required has been suggested by one American judge: "The modern lawyer almost invariably advises his client upon not only what is permissible but also what is desirable. . . . His duty to society as well as to his client involves many relevant social, economic, political and philosophical considerations."[7] Often the challenge cannot be met by one man alone. The complexity of American law and the flexible and malleable character of American business organizations make a specialized knowledge of many fields as well as a substantial library increasingly necessary. Today the giant law firm can be found in many cities in the form of a partnership with a total complement of as many as several dozen partners and two or three times as many associates. Although generally speaking each client looks to one particular partner as his lawyer, there are partners specializing in such fields as taxation, corporation law, antitrust law, real estate transactions, and litigation. They claim a goodly share of the business of the giants of industry and commerce, whose problems seem to call for the cooperation of specialists, and each year they hire many of the top graduates of the leading law schools. These young men do much of the painstaking legal research and while they hope for partnership, they know that, in any case, after five or six years of experience as an associate in such a firm, other attractive opportunities will be open to them. Even outside of the relatively small number of such large firms, specialization is becoming more common, with lawyers whose practice consists largely or exclusively, for example, of personal injury cases, tax matters, or labor cases. These same changes have brought about an increase in the number of lawyers engaged in another branch of the profession as house or corporate counsel.

House or Corporate Counsel

Out of every twenty lawyers, two are house or corporate counsel—salaried lawyers in the employ of private business concerns, usually industrial corporations, insurance companies, and banks. The growth of corporations, the complexity of business, and the multitude of problems posed by government regulation make it desirable for such firms to have in their employ men with legal training who, at the same time, are intimately fami-

---

[7] Judge Wyzanski in *United States* v. *United States Shoe Machinery Corp.*, 89 F. Supp. 357, 359 (D. Mass. 1950).

liar with the particular problems and conditions of the firm. The proportion of the profession engaged in this kind of activity can be expected to increase in coming years. Counsel is usually an officer of the company and may serve on important policy making committees and perhaps even on the board of directors. He remains a member of the bar and is entitled to appear in court although an outside lawyer is often retained for litigation as well as some other matters. However, it is the house or corporate counsel's skill as advisor rather than as advocate which makes him a valued asset. He is constantly in touch with his employer's problems, is ideally situated to practice preventive law, and may also be called upon to advise his company on its broader obligation to the public and the nation.

LAWYERS IN GOVERNMENT

A parallel development has taken place in government and two out of twenty lawyers are now employees of the federal, state, county, and municipal governments, exclusive of the judiciary. Many of those entering public service are recent law graduates who find government salaries sufficiently attractive at this stage of their careers and seek the training which such service may offer as a prelude to private practice. Limitations on top salaries discourage some from continuing with the government, although in recent years public service has become more attractive as a career. The majority serves by appointment in the legal departments of a variety of federal and state agencies and local entities. The United States Department of Justice alone employs more than sixteen hundred, and the Law Department of the City of New York more than three hundred. Others are engaged as public prosecutors. Federal prosecutors, the United States attorneys and their assistants, are appointed by the President and are subordinate to the Attorney General of the United States. State prosecutors, sometimes known as district attorneys, are commonly elected by each county and are not under the control of the state attorney general. As a rule, lawyers in government are directly engaged in legal work, since law training is infrequently sought as preparation for general government service. However, a small but important minority which constitutes an exception to this rule consists of those who have been appointed to high executive positions and those who have been elected to political office. For one hundred and seventy years, lawyers have made up about two thirds of the United States Senate, one half of the House of Representatives, and between one half and two thirds of the state governors. These figures bear out the comment of Chief Justice Stone that, "No tradition of our profession is more cherished by lawyers than that of its leadership in public affairs."

JUDGES

Fewer than one in twenty of those admitted to practice law is a federal, state, county, or municipal court judge. Except for some inferior courts, judges are generally required to be admitted to practice but do not practice while on the bench. There is so little uniformity that it is difficult to generalize further than to point out three salient characteristics which relate to the ranks from which judges are drawn, to the method of their selection, and to their tenure.

Judges are drawn from the practicing bar, and less frequently from government service or the teaching profession. There is in the United States no career judiciary such as is found in many other countries and there is no prescribed route for the young law graduate who aspires to be a judge, no apprenticeship which he must serve, no service which he may enter. The outstanding young law graduates who act for a year or two as law clerks to the most distinguished judges of the federal and state courts have only the reward of the experience to take with them into practice and not the promise of a judicial career. While it is not uncommon for a vacancy on a higher court to be filled by a judge from a lower court, even this cannot be said to be the rule. The legal profession is not entirely unaware of the advantages of a career judiciary, but it is generally thought that they are outweighed by the experience and independence which American lawyers bring to the bench. Many of the outstanding judges of the country's highest courts have had no prior judicial experience. Criticism has centered instead about the prevalent method of selection of judges.

In over two thirds of the states, judges are elected, usually by popular vote, but occasionally by the legislature.[8] Popular

---

[8] It has not always been so. The first state constitutions generally provided for selection of judges either by the legislature or by the governor, or both, and for life tenure. This system was swept away during the wave of Jacksonian democracy in the middle of the nineteenth century and the change was made to popular vote and short judicial terms.

election has been the subject of much disapproval, including that of the American Bar Association, on the ground that the public lacks interest in and information on candidates for judicial office and that therefore the outcome is too often controlled by leaders of political parties. The situation has been somewhat improved since many local bar associations have undertaken to evaluate the qualifications of candidates and to support or oppose them on this basis. Since 1937, however, the American Bar Association has advocated the substitution of a system under which the governor appoints judges from a list submitted by a special nominating board and the judge then periodically stands unopposed for reelection by popular vote on the basis of his record. Such a system is now in effect in several states. In another small group of states, judges are appointed by the governor subject to legislative confirmation. This is also the method of selection of federal judges, who are appointed by the President subject to confirmation by the Senate.[9] Even under the appointive system the selection of judges is not immune from political influence and appointees are usually of the President's or governor's own party. But names of candidates for the federal judiciary are submitted to a committee of the American Bar Association and appointment is usually made only with its approval. The office of chief judge or chief justice is usually filled in the same manner as other judicial offices, although in some states it is filled from among the members of the court by rotation, by seniority of service, or by vote of the judges. The Chief Justice of the United States is appointed by the President, subject to Senate confirmation.

The third characteristic is that judges commonly serve for a term of years rather than for life. For courts of general jurisdiction it is typically four or six years, and for appellate courts, six or eight years. Happily, even where selection is by popular election, it is customary to return to office sitting judges whose service has been satisfactory. In a few state courts and in the federal courts the judges sit for life. Whether on the bench for a term of years or for life, a judge may be removed from office only for gross misconduct and only by formal proceedings. Instances of removal have been rare indeed and only four federal

---

[9] District court appointments are subject to a rule of senatorial courtesy under which a senator from the President's own party must approve appointments within his state. Refusal to confirm is rare, and only once in this century has a nominee for the Supreme Court been rejected by the Senate.

judges have ever been removed by formal proceedings.[10] The independence of the judiciary is also encouraged by the rule that a judge incurs no civil liability for his judicial acts, even if he is guilty of fraud and corruption. A number of states have canons of ethics to which judges are expected to adhere and the Canons of Judicial Ethics of the American Bar Association are generally respected even where they have not been formally adopted. Salaries for the higher judicial offices are usually good although less than the income of a successful private practitioner, the prestige of these offices is high, and the bench has been able to attract many of the country's ablest legal minds. The great names in American law are in large part the names of its great judges.

LAW TEACHERS

American law teachers, like American judges, serve no formal apprenticeship before their appointment, and like judges, they are often drawn from the practicing bar. Their most common titles are assistant professor, associate professor, and professor. Although graduate study or a period as a teaching fellow is not uncommon as preparation for a teaching career in law, neither is essential nor even usual. Less than one third of the law faculties at Columbia, Harvard, and Yale, for example, have earned doctorate degrees.[11] In spite of the practical background of many law teachers, the leading law schools, with few exceptions, demand that the members of their faculties devote their full time to teaching and research and give up the regular practice of law. American law teachers seem to be given to introspection and the attention which they pay to the educational process itself is probably unsurpassed in any other country. One of the striking characteristics of the American law faculty is the independence of even its youngest members of their senior colleagues. Each man teaches his own courses, and prepares and grades his own examinations. None is under the supervision of another,[12] and the academic freedom of each is jeauously guarded.

---

[10] In 1804, 1862, 1912, and 1936. Federal judges are removed by impeachment proceedings in the Senate. Judges have, on occasion, resigned rather than face impeachment.

[11] It must be remembered, however, that the degree of bachelor of laws usually evidences seven years of university education.

[12] The "chairs" which are occupied by distinguished professors at many American law schools may carry honor and stipend, but give no supervisory responsibility over other faculty members or scholars.

PROFESSIONAL ORGANIZATIONS

Bar associations had existed in colonial times and through the first few decades of the nineteenth century, but they fell into disuse long before the middle of the century and the history of the revival of lawyer's professional organizations in the United States can be dated from 1870. In that year the Association of the Bar of the City of New York was organized for the immediate purpose of fighting corruption in local government. It set the pattern for such organizations for the next fifty years: it was unofficial, voluntary, selective in its membership, and included only a small fraction of the members of the profession in New York City. It remains today one of the most influential and active. By 1923 every state and territory had a bar organization and by 1930 city and county groups were said to number over one thousand. Their purposes include reforming and unifying the law, improving the administration of justice, advancing legal education, upholding the standards of the profession, providing continuing legal education for their members, increasing the availability of legal services, and furnishing library facilities. In 1878 the first and most important of the nationwide associations, the American Bar Association, was formed on the pattern of the Association of the Bar of the City of New York. Although one of its objectives was to coordinate and correlate the activities of the entire organized bar, it is a separate entity rather than a true federation of state or local organizations. Its membership was at first highly selective, and while it has made efforts to broaden its base, it still includes less than one half of those admitted to the practice of law in the country.

It was not until 1921 that the first state, by legislation patterned after a model act recommended by the American Bar Association and the American Judicature Society, required that every lawyer be a dues-paying member of the state bar association. Such a bar is said to be "integrated." About half of the states now have integrated bars, which give the profession a way to express its opinions as a body. One purpose of integration is to improve the discipline of lawyers in relations with their clients, a matter which traditionally has been handled by the high court of the state. Disciplinary measures may include fines and imprisonment for contempt of court, censure, suspension, and disbarment. Fewer than eighty out of the quarter million American lawyers are disbarred each year. In 1956 the American

Bar Association approved a set of Model Rules of Court for Disciplinary Proceedings. In almost all of the integrated states the bar has an investigatory function in disciplinary proceedings and in many it has a trial function as well, leaving the courts with only a power of review. In non-integrated states voluntary bar associations have rarely been given functions in disciplinary matters. Generally the integrated states also have official canons of professional ethics patterned after those promulgated by the American Bar Association. Most non-integrated states do not.

Aside from the general professional organizations, a number of groups seek to serve special needs, and of these two are particularly worthy of mention: the American Law Institute and the American Judicature Society. The American Law Institute was organized in 1923 to overcome the uncertainty and complexity of American law. It is a select group of about fifteen hundred lawyers, judges, and law teachers, whose projects have included the Restatement of the Law, uniform and model laws, and educational programs mentioned elsewhere. The American Judicature Society was established in 1913 to promote the efficient administration of justice. It has promulgated model acts in this field and has worked for an integrated bar.

AVAILABILITY OF LEGAL SERVICES

One of the objects of many bar associations is to increase the availability of legal services, particularly to segments of society that have difficulty in affording such services. It has been estimated that twenty percent of those in metropolitan areas are in this category. Legal assistance in civil cases is furnished the neediest at no cost or at a token cost by legal aid societies, supported largely by voluntary contributions. They are organized locally and joined in a federation by the National Legal Aid and Defender Association. Some of its offices are operated directly by local bar associations, and the American Bar Association actively cooperates with and supports the National Legal Aid and Defender Association. Legal aid has grown remarkably since its beginnings near the end of the last century. By 1920 there were thirty-three legal aid offices; by 1949 the number had increased to ninety-two; and by 1960 to two hundred and nine. Legal assistance to those who can afford to pay something is often handled through lawyer-reference plans in which anyone may be referred to a competent and reliable lawyer who is available for consultation for a moderate fee and who will render further service if needed. A lawyer's fee is a matter to be arranged between himself and his client, although in some communities bar associations have adopted schedules of fees as guides to what is considered reasonable. Furthermore the contingent fee[13] is generally permitted and often enables claimants to obtain counsel in personal injury cases. And in many cities there are small claims courts, with jurisdiction in most civil matters up to several hundred dollars and an informal procedure in which costs are minimal and a lawyer is not needed. In criminal prosecutions, depending on the place and type of case, several systems are used to provide counsel for those unable to pay: counsel may be assigned by the court without compensation; counsel may be assigned by the court and compensated from public funds; a full time public official may be made available through a public defender system; or a lawyer may be furnished through a voluntary or private defender system or legal aid. Special provision may be made to reduce the cost of appealing an adverse decision in either a criminal or civil case if the losing party is a needy person. But while great advances have been made in both civil and criminal cases, more needs to be done to make adequate assistance available to all.

Continuing Legal Education

Another objective of bar associations has been to provide for the continuing legal education of the profession. A pioneer in this field has been Practising Law Institute in New York City, a nonprofit educational corporation, which serves over ten thousand lawyers a year with evening lecture courses, Saturday forums, and summer sessions. Since 1947 the American Law Institute and the American Bar Association have collaborated through a joint committee which supervises post admission legal education programs throughout the nation and has published suitable materials for this purpose. Both bar associations and law schools sponsor lectures and institutes on professional topics and in several states active programs are run jointly by the bar and the schools. Continuing legal education has rapidly

---

13 A contingent fee is fixed as a percentage of the client's recovery. In the event that there is no recovery, no fee is due.

expanded since the Second World War and promises to continue its growth in coming years.

Suggested Readings

An extensive survey of the legal profession in the United States is summarized in Blaustein and Porter, *The American Lawyer* (1954). Other helpful sources are: Cheatham, *Cases and Materials on the Legal Profession* (1955), a casebook with useful notes and other materials; Hurst, *The Growth of American Law: The Law Makers,* Chapters 7, 12, 13 (1950), a history of law including the legal profession; and Mayers, *The American Legal System,* Chapter 12 (1955), a textbook for college students. A volume of *Selected Readings on the Legal Profession* (1962) has been assembled under the auspices of the Association of American Law Schools. Another collection of readings is Countryman, *The Lawyer in Modern Society* (1962).

Chapter IV

The Judicial System

*A salient characteristic of the American judicial establishment is
its cleavage into parallel systems of state and federal courts. How
are these systems organized and what are the limits of their jurisdiction?*

STATE COURTS

For the most part, law in the United States can be con-
veniently classified, according to its sources, as decisional law
and legislation. Custom, a third possibility, is relatively insignificant as a source of law. It may be used, for example, in interpreting a contract or in determining whether a prescribed
standard of conduct has been met, but rarely has it given rise to
a new legal rule.[1] The judicial system is the most appropriate
starting point for an inquiry into the sources of law for, although decisional law stands below legislation in the hierarchy
of authorities and case law is subject to change by statute, the
judiciary has been the traditional fountainhead of law in America as in other common law countries. One of the results of the
particular form of federalism which has grown up in the United
States is a judicial structure in which a nationwide system of
federal courts functions alongside the courts of the fifty states.

The great bulk of all litigation comes before the state
courts.[2] Each state by constitution and statute has established
its own system, and the lack of uniformity makes it impossible
to give a detailed description to fit all states. Too often the state

---

[1] But see p. 10 *supra* for an example of the use of custom as a source of water
and mining law.

[2] In a recent decade state appellate court decisions filled nearly six hundred
volumes in the unofficial reports while federal appellate court opinions filled just
over one hundred volumes.

courts bear the stamp of conditions and concepts belonging to the time of their origins and long since changed or outmoded. In the late eighteenth century, when the first court systems were established, travel was difficult and communication was slow. The response was to create a number of courts of general jurisdiction to bring justice close to the people, who soon came to regard the state court in their locality as their own particular possession. This policy of multiplication of courts and decentralization of the court system has persisted until modern times. In recent years, however, considerable progress has been made in the simplification of state court systems and the improvement of judicial administration, partly through the efforts of the American Judicature Society and the judicial councils organized by many states to evaluate their judicial system and make improvements.

In each state there are trial courts of general jurisdiction which are called by such names as district, superior, or circuit courts or courts of common pleas.[3] A single judge presides, whether there is a jury or not, and is generally competent to hear all cases, civil and criminal, which are not restricted to special courts or divisions. Such special courts or divisions with limited jurisdiction may include criminal courts, family or domestic relations courts, juvenile or children's courts, and probate or surrogates' courts for decedents' estates. In addition there are courts of inferior jurisdiction which handle petty matters. These were traditionally the justice of the peace courts, but they have often been supplanted by county, municipal, small claims, police, and traffic courts. Neither at the state nor the federal level are there special administrative or commercial courts such as exist in some countries.

At the top of the state judicial system is the highest appellate court of that state.[4] In most states it is called simply the supreme court; in some it is known by another name, such as the court of appeals in New York and in several other states. The number of judges ranges from three to nine, with seven the most common number, including a chief justice and associate justices. The growing number of appeals has produced two devices to

---

[3] Circuit courts are so called because at one time judges traveled about "on circuit" to hold court. In New York the court of general jurisdiction is known as the Supreme Court, Trial Term.

[4] In Oklahoma and Texas there are two high courts, one for civil appeals and the other for criminal appeals.

handle the increased business of the state appellate courts. In some states the highest court sits in separate divisions, or panels, each with general jurisdiction and with provision for the resolution of inconsistencies among the decisions of these divisions. In others there are intermediate appellate courts, usually called courts of appeal or appellate courts,[5] between the courts of general jurisdiction and the highest court. In the largest number of states, however, there is neither a separate division of the highest court nor an intermediate appellate court.

FEDERAL COURTS

The decision of the framers of the Constitution to leave to Congress the creation of lower federal courts, if any there should be, has given flexibility and the opportunity for experiment to the federal judicial system. This system has three principal levels: the district courts, the courts of appeals, and the Supreme Court. There are also such special courts of limited jurisdiction as the Court of Claims,[6] the Customs Court, the Court of Customs and Patent Appeals, and the Court of Military Appeals. Although there is no special system of administrative courts, there are, to be sure, many federal administrative tribunals which have adjudicatory functions, but which are not properly courts.[7]

The district courts are the trial courts of general jurisdiction for both civil and criminal cases and may sit as bankruptcy or admiralty courts as well. They also review the decisions of some federal administrative agencies. There are eighty-six district courts located throughout the fifty states. Some states contain only one judicial district, while other are divided into as many as four judicial districts. The territorial jurisdiction of a district court extends, with some exceptions, only within the state where it is located. Although a judicial district may have a number of judges, depending on the volume of cases, a single judge generally presides over both jury and non-jury cases. In some special cases the court must consist of three judges, one of whom must be a member of a higher federal court.

Appeals from a district court are generally heard in the

---

[5] In New York, where the Court of Appeals is the high court, the intermediate appellate court is called the Appellate Division of the Supreme Court.

[6] The Court of Claims hears certain claims against the United States.

[7] On judicial control of administrative actions, see p. 150 *infra*.

court of appeals for the circuit in which the district is located, although in rare instances appeal may be directly to the Supreme Court. There are eleven such circuits, ten comprising geographical divisions of the states and including a number of districts and an eleventh for the District of Columbia. These are the intermediary appellate courts in the federal system, but because of the limitations on review by the Supreme Court they are, in fact, the courts of last resort for most federal cases. In addition to hearing appeals from the district courts, they also review decisions of certain federal administrative agencies such as the National Labor Relations Board. The number of judges in each circuit varies, but the judges ordinarily hear appeals in panels of three.

Appellate review of the decisions of the courts of appeals is in the hands of the Supreme Court, which since 1869 has consisted of nine men, one chief justice and eight associate justices, who sit as a body and not in panels. Their number is fixed by Congress.[8] It is the only federal court created by the Constitution; all others are creatures of congressional enactment under a grant of power in the Constitution. As will be explained shortly, it is not only the highest appellate court of the federal system, but also has a limited power of review over the state courts. However, the proportion of cases in which either sort of review is in fact allowed is very small.

Federal Jurisdiction

The determination of the jurisdiction of the state and federal courts is a part of the more general problem of the distribution of state and federal power. Under the Constitution, the federal government has only those powers which are granted to it, and the residual powers are left to the states or to the people. Whatever judicial jurisdiction has not been given exclusively to the federal courts remains in the state courts, and it is therefore customary to discuss the division of judicial power in terms of federal, rather than state, jurisdiction.

Because the federal district courts were created by congressional enactment, their jurisdiction is defined not only by the constitutional grant of federal judicial power but also by the

---

[8] The most recent attempt to change the number of judges on the Supreme Court came in 1937, when President Franklin Delano Roosevelt proposed what came to be known as his "court-packing" bill, in response to Supreme Court decisions holding parts of his legislative program unconstitutional.

implementation of that power by federal legislation which began with the First Judiciary Act of 1789. Congress need not grant, and indeed has not granted, jurisdiction to the district courts to the full extent of the power given it by the Constitution. The criminal jurisdiction of the district courts, which accounts for a substantial minority of all cases, includes all offenses against federal law. Most of the civil business of these courts is of three kinds: first, cases in which the United States is a party; second, cases between private parties involving federal laws, under the so-called "federal question" jurisdiction; and third, cases between citizens of different states, under the so-called "diversity" jurisdiction. The first category embraces actions brought "by the United States, or by an agency or officer thereof expressly authorized to sue by Act of Congress" and certain actions against the United States in which Congress has conferred jurisdiction upon the district courts. Its reason should be evident. The second category, cases under federal question jurisdiction, consists of controversies arising under the Constitution, laws, or treaties of the United States, generally where the amount in controversy exceeds $10,000. The federal courts are thus charged with the vindication of federally created rights. The third category, diversity jurisdiction, comprehends cases where the dispute is between citizens of different states including foreign states, and the amount in controversy exceeds $10,000.[9] Its justification is not entirely clear. The conventional explanation is that the framers of the Constitution sought to avoid the partiality which might result if, for example, a New York creditor were obliged to try his claim against a Massachusetts debtor before a Massachusetts state court. In any event, litigants' preference for the federal courts today comes less from a fear of prejudice than a belief that the court, the procedure, or the court calendar is more favorable. Diversity jurisdiction has come under fire from time to time and remains the most controversial ground of federal judicial power.

In some cases Congress has made the jurisdiction of the federal courts exclusive. Thus in cases under the federal criminal laws, some admiralty or maritime cases, bankruptcy proceedings, and cases under patent or copyright laws, the matter cannot be brought before a state court. In most cases it has not

---

[9] For the purpose of determining whether there is diversity, a corporation is regarded as a citizen not only of the state where it has been incorporated but also of the state where it has its principal place of business.

done so and jurisdiction of federal and state courts is concurrent, which means that the plaintiff can bring his action in either. Cases of diversity jurisdiction and many cases of federal question jurisdiction are instances of concurrent jurisdiction. Thus state created rights may be enforced in the federal courts and federally created rights may be enforced in the state courts. Where jurisdiction is concurrent and suit has been brought in the state court, however, the defendant usually has the right to have the case removed to the federal district court. In these cases of concurrent jurisdiction, either party may select the federal courts, the plaintiff by his original choice of forum and the defendant by removal[10]

Under the Constitution, the Supreme Court itself has original, or trial, jurisdiction over a few categories of cases, the most usual being disputes among the states themselves. The trial is conducted by an officer of the court known as a special master who is appointed for that case and who reports his findings to the Court. However, such cases are not common. Its jurisdiction is in the main appellate and is determined, within constitutional limits, by Congress. The mechanism of review is designed to limit those cases decided on the merits with full consideration to a relatively small and manageable number, which are usually of some concern to the public at large as well as to the litigants. Thus while the Court may dispose of upwards of two thousand cases a year, it decides less than fifteen percent of them on the merits and only about one-half of this smaller number with full opinions.

One of the most important limitations on the work of the Supreme Court, as well as the lower federal courts, is that its jurisdiction extends only to "cases and controversies." It will only decide lawsuits between adversary litigants who have real interests at stake in a ripened controversy. It will not give advisory opinions, even on constitutional questions, and even at

---

[10] There are some exceptions. A resident defendant who is sued in a state court by a non-resident plaintiff cannot remove on the ground of diversity.

[11] However the Supreme Court has held constitutional the Declaratory Judgment Act. of 1934 which authorizes federal courts, under certain circumstances including the existence of an "actual controversy", to render a judgment declaring the rights of the parties in advance of any claim for damages. *Aetna Life Insurance Co.* v. *Haworth*, 300 U.S. 227 (1937). The highest courts of several of the states are empowered to give advisory opinions to the state legislature or executive.

the request of the President or Congress.[11] Another restriction is that federal questions must be "substantial" in order to confer jurisdiction on the Supreme Court. And in no event will the Court review decisions of the state courts on questions of state law. The state courts are themselves the final arbiters of state law and their decisions are conclusive on such matters.

Congress has provided for two principal methods of review by the Supreme Court: by appeal and by writ of certiorari. Appeal is a matter of right. It lies from a state court of last resort which has held a state statute to be valid in spite of a contention that it is repugant to the Constitution or other federal law, or which has, in a rare case, held a federal statute or treaty to be invalid. In exceptional situations it also lies from a lower federal court. But in most cases, review may be had, if at all, only upon a writ of certiorari, a command issued from the Supreme Court to the lower federal court or the state court of last resort[12] requiring it to certify and return the record of the proceedings in the case. Even in a proper case, the issuance of such a writ is within the discretion of the Court.[13] It may be granted upon the petition of a party to any case before a federal court of appeals. It may also be granted to review a judgment of a state court of last resort where, for example, a state statute has been held to be invalid under the Constitution or other federal law or where a right is claimed under the Constitution or other federal law. But certiorari will only be granted for "special and important reasons" and the fact that the decision below is erroneous is not such a reason. Circumstances which may influence the Court to grant certiorari include the existence of a conflict in decisions among federal courts of appeals for different circuits, or between a decision by a state court on a federal question and the decisions of the Supreme Court itself. While the bulk of the cases disposed of annually by the Court consists of some fifteen hundred requests for certiorari, it grants only about ten percent of these and rejects the remainder as unsuitable for review.[14]

---

12 By this is meant the highest state court to which the case could be taken on appeal. It is usually, although not always, the highest court of the state.

13 It is the practice to grant certiorari only on the concurrence of at least four justices.

14 A survey of the work of the court during the preceding year appears annually in the *Harvard Law Review*.

LAW APPLIED IN THE FEDERAL COURTS

Because the federal government has only such powers as are conferred upon it by the Constitution, federal law is supreme only in limited areas. It is generally interstitial and rarely occupies a field completely, so that litigation in American courts often involves complex problems of accommodation of state and federal law. In either a state or federal court, an action based on a right derived from state law may be met by a defense based on federal law, or conversely one based on federal law may be met by a defense based on state law. The federal courts are thus frequently called upon to apply state law, and while the problem of giving effect in one jurisdiction to the laws of another is not, to be sure, peculiar to American federalism, the role of state law in the federal courts has had a unique history.

In 1842, in the landmark case of *Swift* v. *Tyson*,[15] the Supreme Court recognized the duty of the federal courts to give effect, on questions within the law-making competence of the states, to state law which was distinctively "local" in character, such as state statutes, decisions construing state statutes, and decisions relating to real property or embodying local customs. But where the state law was considered to be "general law" —by which the Court meant the general provisions of the common law—the federal courts were under a duty to ascertain the relevant legal principles independently, from reason and authority, and they were to apply these principles even though the courts of the particular state would have acted upon a different understanding of the "general law". Thus there grew up what was in effect a "federal common law", binding upon the federal courts but not upon the state courts, and the outcome of litigation might depend upon which court, state or federal, heard the case. Critics deplored the "forum shopping" that ensued, as well as the frustration of state policies in cases involving no federal interest other than that in providing a forum for controversies between citizens of different states. Defenders of the decision maintained that it contributed towards a needed national uniformity in the law.

In 1938, when the doctrine of *Swift* v. *Tyson* had been in force for almost a century, it was overruled by the Supreme Court in *Erie Railroad Co.* v. *Tompkins*.[16] The opinion of the

[15] 41 U.S. (16 Pet.) 1 (1842).
[16] 304 U.S. 64 (1938).

Court in this historic case, by Justice Brandeis,[17] rested finally upon the constitutional ground that in areas reserved by the Constitution to the states, the federal courts were bound to apply state case law no less than state statute law. This decision has in turn given rise to a host of new problems. The Supreme Court has interpreted the principle of the case as requiring, in cases of diversity jurisdiction, that a federal court adjudicating claims arising under state law arrive at substantially the same outcome as would a court of the state in which it sits. This has brought developments which are novel from the point of view of choice of law. Ordinarily, the forum applies its own rules of choice of law to determine what foreign law, if any, to apply The federal forum giving effect to state law, however, must follow the choice of law principles of the state in which it sits.[18] And although it will apply federal rather than state law as to matters of "procedure", rules that would decisively affect the outcome of the litigation have usually been regarded as "substantive" rather than "procedural".[19] The extent to which the federal courts are bound by the decisions of inferior state courts and the dicta of even the highest state court is a troublesome, although not unique, problem, which is thought by some to be unsuited to the dignity of the federal judiciary. The issues raised by state law in the federal courts are generally complex and still in a state of flux.

SUGGESTED READINGS

There is no single comprehensive work on both the federal and state court systems. The Institute of Judicial Administration has prepared a helpful pamphlet on this subject entitled *A Guide to Court Systems* (1960). Abraham, *The Judicial Process* (1962) is an introductory text. See also Mayers, *The American Legal System*, Chapters 1 and 3 (1955), a textbook for college students, and Murphy and Pritchett, *Courts, Judges, and Politics: An Introduction to the Judicial Process* (1961), a col-

---

[17] Louis Dembitz Brandeis (1858-1941) practiced in Boston, Massachusetts for about forty years after graduation from Harvard Law School. He was appointed an associate justice of the Supreme Court of the United States in 1916, although he had previously held no judicial or other public office. Because of his alleged "radical" position on social and economic issues, his confirmation aroused the most substantial opposition to meet any successful appointee to the Court during this century. He served with great distinction until his retirement in 1939.

[18] *Klaxon* v. *Stentor Electric Manufacturing Co.*, 313 U.S. 487 (1941).

[19] *Guaranty Trust Co.* v. *York*, 326 U.S. 99 (1945).

lection of materials, including cases and introductory text, emphasizing the judicial process in the federal courts, and Scigliano, *The Courts: A Reader in the Judicial Process* (1962), another collection of readings. Hart and Wechsler, *The Federal Courts and the Federal System* (1953) is a leading casebook on federal jurisdiction, with extensive textual notes including historical background. For an elementary summary of the jurisdiction of federal courts, see Bunn, *A Brief Survey of the Jurisdiction and Practice of the Courts of the United States* (5th ed. 1949). Pound, *Organization of Courts* (1940) is an historical study of state courts with suggestions for improvement. A biennial tabulation of information on state governments is contained in Council of State Governments, *The Book of the States,* 1962-63, Section III: The Judiciary (1962).

Chapter V

Case Law

Case law has special significance in the United States because of the common law tradition. What is its form, where can it be found, and what authority does it have?

FORM OF REPORTED CASES

Because of the doctrine of precedent, some knowledge of the form of reported cases is particularly important to an understanding of American law. Case law is found primarily in the decisions of appellate courts; except for the federal trial courts, and those of a few states, trial court opinions are not published. The typical case is entitled by the names of the parties, for example, *Jones* v. *Smith*. Usually the name which appears first is that of the original plaintiff in the trial court, but in some jurisdictions it is that of the party taking the appeal. A criminal case may appear as *State* v. *White* or *Green* v. *United States*. Occasionally, particularly in non-adversary proceedings such as bankruptcy, only one name appears, as *In re Brown* or *Ex parte Black*. Following the title will come a headnote or syllabus summarizing the opinion, occasionally a digest of the arguments of counsel, perhaps a statement of the facts by the reporter, and then the portion of the report that carries authority —the opinion of the court followed by its decision disposing of the case.

An opinion may vary in length from less than one to more than twenty pages, but five pages is typical. Although it is the "opinion of the court" it is commonly written on behalf of the court by a single judge, whose name precedes the opinion. He will usually summarize the facts and the procedural history of the case and give a full and careful statement of the reasons for the decision, citing statutes, cases, and other authorities.[1] Judges are expected to have the time to do this. In a year the nine judge Supreme Court of the United States and the seven judge Court of Appeals of New York each write such opinions in well under one hundred and fifty cases. In preparing opinions, a judge may be assisted by a law clerk, usually a high-ranking recent law school graduate who has already had writing experience as a student on one of the law reviews. The decision itself is by majority vote[2] and is stated at the end of the opinion. It may affirm, reverse, or modify the decision of the court below, and may contain directions for further proceedings by the lower court. The members of the court who concur may then be listed. If a judge agrees with the decision but not with the opinion, he may write a separate concurring opinion stating his reasons for concurrence. However, in contrast to the English practice, concurring opinions are the exception rather than the rule in the United States. A judge who disagrees with the decision may dissent, with or without an opinion.[3] Opinions need not be signed, however, and it is not uncommon for a court to write an unsigned and usually shorter opinion *per curiam*—by the ocurt —when, for example, the point in issue is thought to be well settled. In most jurisdictions a court need not give any reasons for its decision, and many appeals, particularly upon affirmance, are disposed of without opinion by what are known as memorandum decisions.[4]

Finding Case Law

The sheer number of decisions is an obvious obstacle to finding case law. Reported decisions of the Supreme Court of the United States and of most of the state appellate courts can be

---

[1] A judge in writing an opinion may well be influenced by his experience at the bar and individual literary styles vary considerably.

[2] If an even number of judges should sit, perhaps because of the disqualification of one, and a tie vote results, the decision of the lower court is thereby affirmed.

[3] The dissent has become peculiarly frequent in the Supreme Court of the United States. The percentage of non-unanimous decisions among those with full opinion has risen from 11% in 1930 to 28% in 1940 to 61% in 1950 to 76% in 1957. See ZoBell, *Division of Opinion in the Supreme Court: A History of Judicial Disintegration*, 44 Corn. L. Q. 186, 205 (1959). Split decisions are less common in the state courts.

[4] In a few states there are statutory or constitutional requirements of written opinions in the appellate courts. See Radin, *The Requirement of Written Opinions*, 18 Calif. L. Rev. 486 (1930).

found in the official reports of those courts. Those decided from at least 1887 to date can also be found in a system of unofficial reports, the National Reporter System, which now contains about 5,000 volumes averaging over 1,000 pages per volume. In this system state court decisions are published in seven sets of volumes, each covering a geographical area of the country, plus two additional sets devoted solely to decisions of the New York and California courts. Federal decisions are published in four sets, one each for the Supreme Court, the courts of appeals, and the district courts, and one for decisions involving the federal rules of procedure.[5] Decisions of the latter two courts are not published officially.[6] Opinions as reported in the unofficial reports are sometimes preferred by lawyers because they are available sooner through publication in temporary pamphlets known as advance sheets, are coordinated with the most comprehensive digest system, and are more compact. A second and highly selective system of unofficial reports, the American Law Reports, publishes only that small fraction of all reported cases which is thought to be of special interest and appends extensive annotations which discuss and cite related cases. It is usual, when referring to a case, to cite both official and unofficial reports. Thus a correct citation would be *Manning v. Noa,* 345 Mich. 130, 76 N.W. 2d 75, 77 A.L.R. 2d 955 (1956), meaning that the case was decided in 1956, is found at page 130 in volume 345 of the official Michigan reports, at page 75 of volume 76 of the second series of the Northwestern set of the National Reporter System, and at page 955 of volume 77 of the second series of American Law Reports, where it is followed by an annotation. In this manner are collected the approximately 30,000 reported court decisions which each year add to the existing total of roughly three million.

This flood of cases is manageable only because of two well developed systems, one of digests and the other of citators. The American Digest System, the leading digest, is coordinated with the National Reporter System, and covers appellate court reports from 1658 to the present. The several points in an

---

[5] Most of the thirteen sets of the National Reporter System are now in a second series of numeration.

[6] Decisions of the Supreme Court of the United States may be found not only in the official United States reports, and the unofficial National Reporter System Supreme Court reports, but in a second series of unofficial reports, the Lawyers' Edition reports.

opinion are digested in short paragraphs and are then numbered and classified by subject matter according to an elaborate classification scheme. The numbered digest paragraphs are printed as the headnotes to the cases as they are reported in the National Reporter System and are also collected in a series of analytically arranged digest volumes. Subject to the vagaries of the classification system, one trained in the use of these digest volumes can, in a relatively short time, collect all of the reported cases, with a few minor exceptions, decided by the courts upon a particular point. The System also includes an alphabetical table of case names. Shepard's Citations, the principal citator, covers the National Reporter System and the official state reports. It indexes decisions which have been cited in later opinions so that in a few minutes it is possible to compile a reasonably complete list of subsequent opinions in which any particular decision has been mentioned.

Rulings and opinions of administrative agencies are harder to find. Although Shepard's Citations covers the decisions of some agencies, they are not reported or indexed in the National Reporter System. The most important federal regulatory agencies publish their own sets of reports and unofficial loose-leaf services, usually in special fields, also contain agency opinions.

The Judicial Function

A judicial decision has two functions in a common law system. The first, which is not, to be sure, peculiar to the common law, is to define and to dispose of the controversy before the court, for under the doctrine of *res judicata* the parties may not relitigate issues that have been determined between them by a valid judgment. This the court must do. It can not abdicate its duty even should the case be a novel one for which there is no controlling authority. The older view was that the court in such a contingency was to discover the law among the principles of the common law, much as a scientist discovers a natural law, and then declare it. Today it is more usual to admit that the court creates the law somewhat as a legislature creates law, but within the narrower bounds set by the facts of the case before it.

Whether the court discovers or creates the law that it applies, its resolution of the controversy has an impact which extends beyond the parties before it. For the second function of a judicial decision, and one that is characteristic of the common law, is that it establishes a precedent so that a like case arising in the future will probably be decided in the same way. This doctrine is often called by its Latin name, *stare decisis*—from *stare decisis et non quieta movere*, to stand by the decisions and not disturb settled points.[7] Reliance on precedent developed early in English law and was received in the United States as part of the tradition of the common law. As a tradition, it has not been reduced to a written rule and is not to be found in constitution, in statute, or even in oath of office.[8] The justifications commonly given for the doctrine may be summarized in the four words: equality, predictability, economy, and respect. The first argument is that the application of the same rule to successive similar cases results in equality of treatment for all who come before the courts. The second is that consistent following of precedents contributes to predictability in future disputes. The third is that the use of established criteria to settle new cases saves time and energy. The fourth is that adherence to earlier decisions shows due respect to the wisdom and experience of prior generations of judges.

For several reasons the doctrine of precedent has never enjoyed in the United States the absolute authority that it is said to have attained in England. The great volume of decisions, with conflicting precedents in different jurisdictions, has detracted from the authority of individual decisions. The rapidity of change has often weakened the applicability of precedents to later cases that have arisen after social and economic conditions have altered with the passage of years. Nevertheless the doctrine of precedent, although less rigidly applied than in England, is still firmly entrenched in the United States.[9]

---

[7] The doctrine of *stare decisis* is used here as synonymous with the doctrine of precedent, and the latter term will generally be employed.

[8] It is reported that the Supreme Court of the United States, where the doctrine of precedent is not at its strongest, overruled itself only ninety times in nearly a century and a half from 1810 to 1957. Blaustein and Field, "Overruling" Opinions in the Supreme Court, 57 Mich. L. Rev. 151 (1958). That the constraint is in the nature of a tradition only is illustrated by the extraordinary example of Judge James E. Robinson, who served as a judge and briefly as chief justice of the Supreme Court of North Dakota, and who attained some notoriety for his disapproval of the doctrine of precedent. Toward the end of his tenure he stated the fact of cases with great brevity and rarely cited authority in his opinions. See Note, 33 Harv. L. Rev. 972 (1920).

[9] It is said that the doctrine is applied by administrative agencies in much the same way as by courts, although its applicability to administrative proceedings is not beyond dispute and may depend upon the nature and functions of the particular tribunal. See Gellhorn and Byse, *Cases and Comments on Administrative Law* 1207 (1960).

TECHNIQUES IN THE USE OF PRECEDENT

Skill in the use of precedent is more art than science. It is no easier to acquire by reading a discussion of the doctrine than it is to learn to ride a bicycle by studying a textbook on mechanics, and the subject matter is considerably more controversial. It is possible, however, to set down the vocabulary, to make some of the more obvious generalizations, and to raise a few of the interesting problems. What follows is, of course, a simplified explanation, which assumes that each case involves only a single "case in point" as a precedent. More often there is a line of decisions, or perhaps several divergent lines, and the task of advocate and court includes the synthesis of a number of cases. In this synthesis may be seen the development and elaboration of a rule, and its broadening or narrowing to meet changing conditions and to take account of the great variety of situations which may arise. Occasionally, at the other extreme, the problem before the court is a novel one, without precedent, and the court must reason from what it conceives to be the public interest and from analogy.

Case law authority is frequently divided into two classes: "persuasive" and "binding." Persuasive authority includes decisions of courts of other jurisdictions and decisions of coordinate courts of the same jurisdiction, for example other intermediate appellate courts of the same state or other federal courts of appeals.[10] The persuasiveness of such a decision may depend on whether it has support in other jurisdictions: when there is a conflict among a number of jurisdictions on a given point, it is common to speak of a "majority" and a "minority" rule and the former may be followed because of its wider acceptance. Or its persuasiveness may depend on the prominence of the court which decided it and of the judge who wrote the opinion: the opinions of such renowned judges as Holmes and Cardozo[11] carry more weight than those of lesser minds. Or its persuasiveness may depend on the similarity of the law and of circum-

---

[10] The authority of state court decisions in the federal courts is discussed in connection with *Erie v. Tompkins*, p. 42 *supra*.

[11] Benjamin Nathan Cardozo (1870-1938) practiced in New York City after graduation from Columbia College and the Columbia School of Law. He served as judge and later chief judge on the Court of Appeals of New York, and was appointed an associate justice of the Supreme Court of the United States in 1932 to fill the vacancy left by Holmes. His best known work is a series of lectures entitled *The Nature of the Judicial Process* (1921).

stances in the two jurisdictions: on a problem of commercial law the courts of the eastern industrial state of New Jersey may be more influenced by a decision from their neighboring eastern industrial state of New York than by a conflicting one from the midwestern agricultural state of Iowa. But in any event, if it is only persuasive authority the doctrine of precedent does not apply and the court is not bound to follow it.

Binding authority, to which the doctrine of precedent does apply, includes decisions of higher courts of the same jurisdiction and decisions of the same court. Since a lower court is not likely to disregard a prior decision of a higher court in the same jurisdiction,[12] which has the power of reversal on appeal, the significant question is the extent to which a court will follow one of its own prior decisions. The question is squarely raised by a single decision, for although the weight of persuasive authority may vary with the number of similar decisions, one of a court's own prior decisions is enough to constitute a precedent. Fundamental to the answer is the distinction between the hold-

---

12 Very rarely, a lower court will decline to follow a decision of a higher court in anticipation that the higher court will overrule its earlier decision if the case is appealed to it. An example is a New York case involving the question of whether a child can recover for breach of warranty (without any proof of fault) for injuries caused by impure food in an action against the retail seller from whom the child's father had purchased the food. Under decisions of the Court of Appeals of New York, the highest state court, in 1923 and 1927, the child could not recover for breach of warranty because the remedy was contractual in nature and since the father made the purchase there was no contract of sale between the retailer and the child. In spite of these precedents, the trial court, the City Court of the City of New York, in 1957 allowed the child to recover. *Greenberg v. Lorenz*, 14 Misc. 2d 279, 178 N.Y.S. 2d 404 (1957). An intermediate appellate court, the Appellate Term of the Supreme Court, affirmed, stating that, "Though it is not within the competence of an intermediate appellate court to disregard controlling precedent, nevertheless when the higher appellate courts—breaking new ground—establish a new trend and render it clear that if the instant question were before them they themselves would overrule earlier pronouncements, it becomes the right, nay the duty, of an intermediate appellate court to take cognizance of it." One of the three judges dissented. *Greenberg v. Lorenz*, 12 Misc. 2d 883, 178 N.Y.S. 2d 407 (1958). A higher intermediate appellate court, the Appellate Division of the Supreme Court, reversed in a short *per curiam* opinion based on precedent. Two of the five judges dissented. *Greenberg v. Lorenz*, 7 A.D. 2d 968, 183 N.Y.S. 2d 46 (1959). But this decision was in turn reversed by the Court of Appeals of New York which reinstated the trial court's judgment for the child and, as the Appellate Term had predicted, overruled the earlier decisions insofar as they applied to the case. *Greenberg v. Lorenz*, 9 N.Y. 2d 195, 173 N.E. 2d 773, 213 N.Y.S. 2d 39 (1961). The court's opinion is set out in the Appendix *infra*. For another example, see Dowling, Patterson, and Powell, *Materials for Legal Method* 240 (2nd ed. by Jones 1952).

ing[13] of a case and the dictum.[14] The distinction stems from the common law's characteristic faith in adversary procedure and the resultant belief that judges, as impartial arbiters, have the competence to decide only those matters which are disputed by the parties and are argued before the court. As to these matters, their decisions are to be treated as precedent and are "binding" authority. But judges, unlike legislators, have no power to lay down rules for cases which are not before them and what they say on such other matters is not binding. In the words of Chief Justice John Marshall, "It is a maxim, not to be disregarded, that general expressions in every opinion, are to be taken in connection with the case in which those maxims are used. If they go beyond the case, they may be respected, but ought not to control the judgment in a subsequent suit when the very point is presented for decision. The reason of this maxim is obvious. The question actually before the court is investigated with care and considered in its full extent. Other principles which may serve to illustrate it, are considered in their relation to the case decided, but their possible bearing on all other cases is seldom completely investigated."[15] It is characteristic of the common law that a point of law may remain unsettled until some losing party determines to assume the burden of presenting that issue in an adversary proceeding on appeal. The holding, then, is the rule of law which was necessary for the decision. Whatever else the judges said that was not necessary to their decision is only dictum.

Dictum is, nevertheless, authority worthy of respect and it would be wrong to assume that it can be disregarded. It may well be followed by the court in later cases; it is often sufficient to persuade a lower court; and it may be regarded by lawyers as a reliable basis for counselling. But it is only persuasive authority and, unlike the holding, is not binding on any court. "Judges," said Justice Cardozo, "differ greatly in their reverence for the illustrations, and comments and side-remarks of their predecessors, to make no mention of their own."[16]

---

[13] In the United States the word "holding" is generally used instead of the term "ratio decidendi," used in England.

[14] The term obiter dictum is also used, often to suggest that the dictum is not reliable.

[15] Marshall made this statement in distinguishing Marbury v. Madison, in which he himself had written the opinion eighteen years earlier. Cohens v. Virginia, 19 U.S. (6 Wheat.) 264, 399 (1821).

[16] Cardozo, The Nature of the Judicial Process 29 (1921).

The holding of a case must be determined from an analysis of the material facts, from the decision, and from the reasoning of the opinion. Even this may be more difficult than would seem at first. It is often hard to know how far the process of abstraction should be continued; to know how broad a statement of the rule is justified. The formulations of rules of law contained in the opinion cannot always be relied upon as authoritative; the rule which the court actually applied may never have been articulated or may have been stated in several different ways in the course of the opinion. Furthermore, the facts may have been stated so concisely that it is hard to tell what they were or in such ample detail that it is difficult to determine which the court thought material. Fortunately no case is decided in isolation and some of these difficulties may be resolved when the opinion is read against the background of other related decisions and general principles.

The rule which the court intended to lay down may not, however, be the holding in the eyes of a later court. When a court is called upon to apply the doctrine of precedent it is faced with not one but two concrete fact situations, that of the earlier decision and that of the case up for decision. With both fact situations in mind, the court derives a rule from the first and decides whether it is applicable to the second, that is, it determines whether the second case is a "like" case. In many instances the precedent gives a decently clear and reasonable rule which the court will apply, more often than not with no inquiry into its merits. At other times, a desirable precedent may not seem to cover an appropriate case or an undesirable precedent may seem to cover an inappropriate case. At this point it should be recognized that the doctrine of precedent does not demand unbending adherence to the past, but admits of more supple techniques which permit an able court to profit from earlier wisdom and experience while rejecting past folly and error. If it seems desirable to extend the principle of a prior decision to the present case, the holding of that decision may be read more broadly than had been intended by the court which handed it down; differences in the facts of the two cases will be treated by the later court as immaterial; and what might have been considered as dictum upon a narrow reading of the earlier case will be regarded as holding. If, on the contrary, it seems undesirable to apply the rule of the earlier decision to the case at hand, the court may narrow the holding of that case in order to distinguish it from the one before it; differences in the facts of the two cases will be treated by the later court as material; and what might have been considered as holding upon a broad reading of the earlier case will be regarded as dictum—as not "necessary" to the disposition of the dispute then before the court. Within certain limits, every decision is subject to such broadening and narrowing. Just where the limits are and just what attitude a given court will take on a given set of facts can be predicted—if at all—only on the basis of experience in working with a tradition that has been handed down through generations of common law students, common law lawyers, and common law judges. As Judge Cardozo put it, "Back of precedents are the basic juridicial conceptions which are the postulates of judicial reasoning, and farther back are the habits of life, the institutions of society, in which these conceptions had their origin, and which, by a process of interaction, they have modified in turn. None the less, in a system so highly developed as our own, precedents have so covered the ground that they fix the point of departure from which the labor of the judge begins. Almost invariably, his first step is to examine and compare them. If they are plain and to the point, there may be need of nothing more. *Stare decisis* is at least the everyday working rule of our law."[17]

But even a decision which is a "binding" authority is not absolutely binding. On rare occasions a court will be faced with a situation in which it cannot render what it regards as a just decision and still stay within what it sees as the limits imposed by the doctrine of precedent. It may resolve the dilemma by following precedent in spite of the injustice in the particular case on the ground that the policies underlying the doctrine outweigh those in favor of the opposite decision. Perhaps it will explain that any change is for the legislature and not the court to make. This result might not be surprising in a case involving commercial law or property law, where predictability is particularly important and where remedial legislative action is generally feasible. On the other hand, the court may be unwilling to follow precedent. The decision may have been clearly wrong when rendered, it may be so old that altered conditions have

---

[17] Cardozo, *The Nature of the Judicial Process* 19-20 (1921).

made it inappropriate,[18] or the composition of the court may have changed so that what was formerly the view of a vehement minority is now that of the majority. For any of these reasons, or for others, the court may refuse to follow precedent and may overrule its earlier decision. This result might not be surprising on a constitutional issue where legislation is not an available remedial device,[19] or on a procedural question, where retroactive change is not exceptional. Tradition demands that where possible the doctrine of precedent be honored by careful distinguishing rather than by outright overruling of objectionable decisions. But in point of fact the decision which has been distinguished and expressly "limited to its particular facts" by a later opinion is often so whittled down as to be virtually overruled.[20]

TWO PUZZLES IN PRECEDENT

Among the puzzling problems that arise out of the doctrine of precedent, two are especially intriguing. The first concerns the weight to be given to a multi-legged holding. It should be apparent that, even among the so-called binding precedents, the value of a decision may be lessened by a number of factors. For example, dissenting or concurring opinions, while they may indicate that the particular judges have hotly disputed the point and are not apt to change their views, usually weaken the authority of a decision and make it less likely that it will be followed by a later court of different composition. Similarly a memorandum decision, which sets forth no reasons, may have effect as precedent if it affirms a decision of a lower court which stated the facts and its reasons in an opinion, but its weight is

---

[18] As in the case of wines, some precedents may improve with age, while others deteriorate. Certainly the accretion of supporting authorities with the passage of time lends strength; on the other hand changing circumstances erode it.

[19] "Stare decisis is usually the wise policy, because in most matters it is more important that the applicable rule of law be settled than that it be settled right. . . . This is commonly true even where the error is a matter of serious concern, provided correction can be had by legislation. But in cases involving the federal Constitution, where correction through legislative action is practically impossible, this Court has often overruled its earlier decisions. The Court bows to the lessons of experience and the force of better reasoning, recognizing that the process of trial and error, so fruitful in the physical sciences, is appropriate also in the judicial function. Justice Brandeis dissenting in Burnet v. Coronado Oil & Gas Co., 285 U. S. 393, 406-08 (1932).

[20] Occasionally a court will simply ignore an embarrassing precedent. This questionable technique leaves the prior decision of doubtful validity in later cases.

much lessened by the circumstance that the higher court gave no reasons for its affirmance of the opinion below.[21] What is the weight of a multi-legged holding—a decision which is based upon several grounds rather than a single ground?

Suppose the case of an appeal from the judgment of a trial court in which three distinct errors are cited as reasons for reversal. Clearly if the appellate court affirms the judgment it has held that each of the three grounds was insufficient, since rejection of each was necessary for affirmance. But suppose that it reverses, stating that the first and second grounds were sufficient but that the third ground was not. What has the court held? Has it held anything as to the first and second grounds? Since either one without the other would have been sufficient for reversal, it can be argued that neither one was necessary to the decision and that there is therefore no holding and the entire opinion is dictum. But each of the points was disputed and was argued before the court and the trial court will be expected to observe both upon any rehearing before it. While neither is the sole ground of the decision, it is usual to treat each as an alternative or multi-legged holding. Yet holdings though they may be, no prudent lawyer can ignore the fact that precedents stand more firmly when they stand on only one leg, and alternate grounds make a holding less reliable. The same words of caution apply with even greater force to the third ground, which was also disputed and was argued before the court and is to be observed by the trial court upon any rehearing, but which was clearly not necessary to the reversal. Whether it be dignified with the name of holding or be classified as dictum, it is obviously an authority of a still lower order than the decision on the first two points.

The second puzzling problem relates to the retroactive effect of a decision which overrules a prior decision. Of course to the extent that a court in reaching any decision announces a new principle of law and applies it to the case already before it there is an aspect of retroactivity, but the effect is particularly apparent where an earlier decision has been overruled. Suppose that two similar transactions have been concluded, one between A and B, the other between C and D. In a dispute between A and B, the highest court of the state decides that such transactions are in-

---

[21] A memorandum decision, however, is valueless as a precedent if the facts of the case cannot be determined.

valid. After this decision, yet a third similar transaction is concluded between E and F. Then in a dispute between C and D, the highest court decides to overrule its earlier decision in the case of A v. B and holds that such transactions are valid. Which decision, that in A v. B or that in C v. D determines the validity of the transaction between E and F, which was concluded in the interval between the two decisions? Is the decision in C v. D retroactive in its effect, or does it apply only to transactions entered into after it was handed down? According to the older theory that judges merely discover existing law and then declare it, the decision of the court in A v. B was simply an erroneous interpretation of what the law was then and still is, an interpretation which was later corrected in C v. D. And since the law was always as stated in C v. D, the transaction between E and F was therefore a valid one, even though it took place before the court had discovered its error. According to the newer theory that judges actually create or make law by their decisions, the decision in A v. B made law that was good law until it was changed in the decision in C v. D. Because the transaction was concluded after the first decision and before the second, during the time when the decision in A v. B was law, the transaction was invalid. Over the years the conflict between these opposing theories has been reflected in conflicting cases, although other considerations may be more important than either theory. Clearly, for example, the case for retroactivity would be weaker if the decision in A v. B had held that the transaction was valid and the decision in C v. D had held that it was invalid. And it would be still weaker if E and F had in fact relied upon the decision in A v. B when entering into their transaction.

The problem of the overruled decision, like that of the multi-legged holding, admits of no simple solution.[22] Occasionally courts, in an attempt to avoid unsetting intervening transactions, have refused to overrule an earlier decision and hold the transaction invalid, but nevertheless have expressed disapproval of the precedent and issued a warning that it would not be followed as to transactions occurring after the decision.[23]

[22] For more on the overruled decision, see Chafee, *Do Judges Make or Discover Law?*, 91 Proc. Am. Philos. Soc. 405 (1947); Lobinger, *Precedent in Past and Present Legal Systems,* 44 Mich. L. Rev. 955 (1946).

[23] *E.g., Hare* v. *General Contract Purchase Corp.,* 220 Ark. 601, 249 S.W. 2d 973 (1952). It has been held that such decisions by a state court do not violate the guarantee of due process in the federal Constitution. *Great Northern Railway* v. *Sunburst Co.,* 287 U.S. 358 (1932).

Suggested Readings

The simplest introductions to case law techniques in the United States are Levi, *An Introduction to Legal Reasoning* (1949), and Morgan, *Introduction to the Study of Law* (2nd ed. with Dwyer 1948). Llewellyn, *The Bramble Bush: On Our Law and Its Study* (1951) is more difficult reading, but is well worth the trouble. A more advanced work on the process of judicial decision by the same author is Llewellyn, *The Common Law Tradition: Deciding Appeals* (1960). There is a discussion of sources of law and judicial precedents in Patterson, *Jurisprudence: Men and Ideas of the Law*, Chapters 9, 11 (1953), an introductory work on legal philosophy. Casebooks with useful collections of textual excerpts are Dowling, Patterson, and Powell, *Materials for Legal Method* (2nd ed. by Jones 1952); Auerbach, Garrison, Hurst, and Mermin, *The Legal Process* (1961); and Fryer and Benson, *Legal Method and System* (one vol. ed. 1950). The most comprehensive manual for legal research is Price and Bitner, *Effective Legal Research: A Practical Manual of Law Books and Their Use* (1953), also available in a revised student edition (1962). Pollack, *Fundamentals of Legal Research* (2nd ed. 1962) is a similar work.

Chapter VI

The Legislative System

In spite of the emphasis on court decisions in a common law system, legislation is of great and increasing importance in American law. What is the hierarchy of authority among the various legislative materials? How do the United States Congress and the fifty state legislatures function? What other special sources of legislation exist?

HIERARCHY OF LEGISLATION

Although case law is traditionally the core of a common law system, legislation has so increased in quantity and importance in the United States during the past century that it is the dominant creative force in many fields. While this is particularly true of federal law,[1] legislation also pours forth from countless lawmaking bodies on the state and local levels. Under the American doctrine of judicial review, the validity of this legislation is a matter for the courts to decide. A court may refuse to apply a legislative enactment to the case before it on the ground that it is invalid because it conflicts with some more authoritative legislative source. For this reason it is important to have an understanding of the hierarchy of these sources.

(1) *The Constitution of the United States.* The Constitution is, to use its own language, the "supreme Law of the Land"

---

[1] In 1947, Justice Felix Frankfurter of the Supreme Court of the United States said: "Inevitably the work of the Supreme Court reflects the great shift in the center of gravity of law-making. Broadly speaking, the number of cases disposed of by opinions has not changed from term to term. But even as late as 1875 more than 40% of the controversies before the Court were common-law litigation, fifty years later only 5%, while today cases not resting on statutes are reduced almost to zero. It is therefore accurate to say that courts have ceased to be the primary makers of law in the sense in which they 'legislated' the common law. It is certainly true of the Supreme Court that almost every case has a statute at its heart or close to it." Frankfurter, *Some Reflections on the Reading of Statutes,* 47 Colum. L. Rev. 527 (1947).

to which all other legislative sources are subject. The ultimate arbiter of constitutional disputes is, of course, the Supreme Court of the United States. Amendments to the Constitution may be proposed by a two-thirds vote of both houses of Congress and must be ratified either by the legislatures of three fourths of the states or by conventions in three fourths of the states.[2] Only twenty-three amendments have been ratified, and of these only thirteen have come since 1791.

(2) *Treaties.* Treaties made by the United States have equal authority with federal statutes, and are subject only to the Constitution. However, in the case of a conflict between a treaty and a subsequent federal statute, the latter controls. A treaty may be entered into by the President with the consent of two thirds of the senators voting, but unless it is a self-executing treaty, it must be implemented by a federal statute before it will take effect as internal law. The President also has limited powers to make executive agreements with foreign nations without the approval of Congress. Such agreements have been given the same effect as treaties by the courts and have, in fact, been more numerous than treaties.

(3) *Federal statutes.* In addition to specifically enumerated legislative powers, the Constitution gives Congress the power to "make all laws which shall be necessary and proper for carrying into execution" the powers expressly vested in any department of the government, and this clause has been broadly construed. The statutes enacted by Congress are, like treaties, subject only to the Constitution, and a statute will be interpreted, if possible, so as to avoid constitutional questions. In the words of Chief Justice Charles Evans Hughes,[3] "We have repeatedly held that as between two possible interpretations of a statute, by one of which it would be unconstitutional and by the other valid, our plain duty is to adopt that which will save the act."[4]

---

[2] All but one of the twenty-three amendments have been ratified by state legislatures rather than conventions.

[3] Charles Evans Hughes (1862-1948) graduated from college at Brown University and in 1884 received a law degree from Columbia University. After practice in New York City, several years as professor of law at Cornell University, and service as special counsel for a state legislative committee, he was elected governor of New York. In 1910 he was appointed an associate justice of the Supreme Court of the United States. In 1916 he ran for President of the United States and, after a narrow defeat by Woodrow Wilson, returned to practice. He subsequently served as Secretary of State of the United States and as a member of the Permanent Court of International Justice. He was appointed Chief Justice of the United States in 1930 and served until ill health forced him to resign in 1941.

[4] *National Labor Relations Board* v. *Jones & Laughlin Steel Corporation*, 301 U.S. 1, 30 (1937).

The process of enactment will be described presently.

(4) *Federal executive orders and administrative rules and regulations.* The Constitution gives to the President a limited power to issue executive orders, which usually are legislative in character and have the effect of federal legislation. Federal administrative bodies may also be empowered to make rules and regulations of a legislative character, which, if validly made pursuant to federal statute, are superior to state legislation.

(5) *State constitutions.* The constitution of a state is subject to valid federal legislation[5] but is the paramount authority within the state itself. State constitutions are often more detailed than the federal Constitution and require more frequent amendment.

(6) *State statutes.* The enactments of state legislatures, while subject to valid federal legislation and to the state constitution, are still of the greatest importance in the many fields of law which have been left to the states. Under the Tenth Amendment to the Constitution, "The powers not delegated to the United States by the Constitution, nor prohibited by it to the States, are reserved to the States respectively, or to the people." Even where Congress has the power to legislate under the Constitution, its power may not be exclusive and the states may have concurrent power, at least where federal legislation has not occupied the field. Since federal legislation is chiefly interstitial in nature, it rarely occupies a field to the exclusion of state law. State statutes are, for the average lawyer, the most common form of legislation. State legislative processes will be discussed shortly .

(7) *State administrative rules and regulations.* Rules and regulations of state administrative bodies, although similar in form and purpose to those of federal agencies, are of less general importance. They may concern such matters as the licensing of various activities within the state.

(8) *Municipal ordinances, rules, and regulations.* Units of local government are extremely varied and are therefore difficult to describe.[6] Each state is divided into counties, which may have legislative powers. Within a county there may be a number of municipalities which are most often governed by an elected mayor and a council. Their enactments, commonly called municipal ordinances, are usually of only local interest. In addi-

[5] Of course, a federal statute must have been enacted under a power granted to Congress in order to prevail over a state constitution or statute.

[6] The delegation to a county or municipality of the power to frame and adopt a charter for self-government is called "home rule." It may be required by the state constitution or may be a product solely of legislative initiative.

tion, local administrative bodies may promulgate rules and regulations.

This, then, is the hierarchy of legislative sources of the law.[7] The remainder of the discussion will be confined to the principal legislative bodies, Congress and the state legislatures.

THE UNITED STATES CONGRESS

Federal statutes are enacted by the United States Congress, a bicameral legislature which consists of a lower house, the House of Representatives, and an upper house, the Senate. The former was intended by the authors of the Constitution to give each state a voice in national affairs proportional to its population. It is made up of 435 members, each of whom is elected for a two-year term by the voters of one of the Congressional Districts into which each state is divided. The number of representatives from a state is determined by federal statute on the basis of its population. The Senate, by contrast, was intended to preserve the equality of the states and voters of each state, regardless of population, elect two senators for a total of one hundred.[8] Senators are elected for six year terms, which are so staggered that only about one third of the total number is elected at each biennial election. Each house serves as a check on the other since legislation requires approval of a majority in both the Senate and the House of Representatives. The life of a Congress is two years commencing in January of odd-numbered years, and each Congress has two regular annual sessions beginning in January. The President may also call a special session if Congress has adjourned.

Because, as will be explained shortly, the history of a federal statute before its enactment may influence a court in construing its language, it is useful to have some knowelge of the legislative process. Most federal legislation takes the form of an Act of Congress, which is introduced in the form of a bill.[9] It

---

7. Rules of court, sometimes considered as a variety of legislation, are discussed at p. 98 *infra*.

8 The senators from the most populous states, New York and California, represent over 50 times as many persons as those from the least populous states, Alaska and Nevada.

9 On occasion a joint resolution is used instead of an act, although there is little practical difference between the two. Congressional legislation, in whatever form, can be divided into "public" and "private" enactments. The latter, enacted for the benefit of a particular individual or group, as for example for the relief of one injured by governmental action, are the more numerous but are of limited interest and this discussion is restricted to "public" laws, which are of general application.

may originate with the member of Congress himself,[10] but more often it will come from his constituents as individuals or as organized groups or from the executive branch. Each house has an Office of Legislative Counsel to aid in the drafting of proposed legislation. Except for bills to raise revenue, which must originate in the House of Representatives, a bill may be introduced in either house, but only by a member of that house.

With rare exceptions it will then as a matter of course be referred to one of the standing committees of the house where it was introduced. Each of the two major parties assigns members to serve on committees, with the larger number going to the majority party and the chairmanship going to the ranking committee member of that party. In some cases subcommittees of the standing committees have been created, which report to the parent committees. Since the workload in Congress is too heavy to permit detailed consideration of every proposal by every member, much of the serious work is done in committee and the committee system is of immense practical significance. Once in committee, the bill may be studied by the experts, on its staff, departments of the executive branch may be requested to submit their views in writing, and if the bill is of sufficient importance there may be public hearings at which interested parties may be heard. Finally the committee members vote to determine the fate of the bill, and either report it favorably with or without amendments, or postpone its consideration by tabling it, which normally prevents further action upon the bill. A large percentage of all bills die in committee.

If the bill is reported favorably, it is customary for the committee to submit a report to Congress with its recommendation. The committee report will rehearse the purpose of the bill, the need for legislation, and the legislative history. It will give a section by section analysis of the bill, an estimate of its cost, reports and comments from appropriate governmental agencies and departments, and may contain minority views in the committee. A verbatim transcript of the hearings is usually published in advance of the committee report. The bill is then brought to the floor of the house for debate, at which time further amendments may be proposed.[11] If the bill is approved by a majority

---

[10] It may also result from an investigation by a House or Senate committee. The power of Congressional committees to investigate stems from the Constitutional grant of "all legislative powers." It is, however, not necessary to the validity of an investigation that legislation actually result.

[11] The proceedings of Congress are published in full in the *Congressional Record*.

vote, it then goes to the other house where a similar procedure of referral to committee followed by debate on the floor is observed. Should the versions passed by both houses be identical, it goes directly to the President for his signature. If there are minor differences, they may be accepted by vote in the house where the bill originated. But should the differences in the two versions be substantial, they must be adjusted by a conference committee consisting of members of both houses, followed by approval of the compromise by a majority vote of each house. The bill is then sent to the President, who has veto power over federal legislation. The President has ten days to sign it into law. If he fails to act within this time the bill becomes law automatically without his signature.[12] If he vetoes the bill it is returned with a veto message stating his reasons to the house where it originated. A two-thirds vote of each house is then necessary to override the veto and enact the bill into law.

State Legislatures

In addition to Congress, each of the fifty states has its own legislative body which is usually termed a "Legislature" or a "General Assembly." These bodies are almost universally bicameral. Although the existence of two houses is often hard to justify except on the basis of tradition going back to colonial times, only one state has changed to a unicameral legislature. The smaller upper house is called the "Senate" and the larger lower house is commonly known as the "House of Representatives." The legislatures range in size from 43 members for the unicameral legislature in Nebraska, and 52 for the bicameral legislature in Delaware, to 424 for the bicameral New Hampshire legislature. Their members are elected for terms of either two or four years, the former being more common for the lower houses and the latter more usual for the senates. Although a majority of states hold sessions only biennially, an increasing number now meets annually. Records of state legislative activity are inadequate compared to congressional records. Hearings and reports of state legislative committees are not usually available nor is any comprehensive record generally kept of statements made during debates on the floor. For this reason a de-

---

[12] However if Congress has adjourned within the ten days, his failure to sign is known as a "pocket veto" and the bill does not become law.

tailed understanding of the mechanics of the legislative process is of less importance in the construction of state than of federal statutes. Although this process is similar to that in Congress, the effectiveness of the committee system and the quality of enactments are impaired by the fact that members of state legislatures, unlike members of Congress, usually do not devote full time to their duties. Technical assistance in drafting legislation is available to committees and individual lawmakers through a legislative reference bureau or library, through a bill drafting staff on the Congressional model, or through the office of the state attorney general. Efforts are being made to improve these services and special commissions may be used to prepare legislation in important fields. Generally the governor, the elected state executive, has veto power over legislation, which can be enacted over his veto only by a two-thirds vote of each house.[13] State, like federal, legislation is subject to judicial review and a state or federal court may refuse to enforce a state statute on the ground of its invalidity.

SPECIAL SOURCES OF LEGISLATION

The role that legislation should play in the common law system of the United States, particularly in those fields of private law which are chiefly the concern of the states, has long been a matter of lively concern. A general trend toward legislation and codification is discernible on the state as well as the federal level. It may be seen in continuous revision of compiled statutes or codes and in special commissions to study and reform broad areas of the law. From the historical point of view, three milestones have been particularly noteworthy: the promulgation of the Field codes between 1848 and 1865, the organization of the National Conference of Commissioners on Uniform State Laws in 1892, and the creation of the New York State Law Revision Commission in 1934.

Following the Revolution, the interest in civil law systems prompted curiosity about the French civil code, which was to have a profound influence on the law of Louisiana. Legislative reform was further stimulated by the writings of Jeremy Ben-

---

13 In a number of states a constitutional provision for initiative and referendum allows the people to propose or enact legislation or requires the submission of certain statutes to the people for their approval.

tham.[14] But the growth of an organized movement toward codification is directly attributable to the struggle of David Dudley
Field of New York.[15] As a result of his efforts, a commission was
established in that state in 1847 to reform civil and criminal
procedure and to codify the law. By 1850, under Field's leadership, complete codes of procedure had been submitted to the
New York legislature and the code of civil procedure had been
adopted. However, at this point the movement lost ground and
in the same year the legislature disbanded the commission. In
1857 Field again succeeded in having the legislature appoint
a commission to codify substantive law. Field personally undertook, with two assistants, the drafting of the civil code. By 1865
the commission submitted its final report with the full text of
five codes: civil procedure, criminal procedure, penal, civil, and
political. New York adopted only Field's first draft of the code
of civil procedure and, in 1881, the code of criminal procedure.
The civil code was passed by the legislature but the governor
vetoed it as the result of opposition by leaders of the bar. A
code of civil procedure which was an elaboration based on his
later draft was adopted between 1876 and 1880. In spite of
their relative lack of success in New York, the influence of the
Field codes was considerable. Some thiry states adopted or
based their codes on the code of civil procedure, which became
a model in the field and profoundly influenced procedural reform.[16] Sixteen states adopted the penal code and the code of
criminal procedure, and five states, including California, adopted and still retain the civil codes. Field's failure to secure more
widespread adoption may have been due in part to the success
of the works of the great nineteenth century text writers, including Kent and Story, in lessening the demand for codification. Perhaps if all of Field's codes had been adopted in New
York, widespread adoption in other states would have followed

14 Jeremy Bentham (1748-1832) was an English jurist and philosopher. He
is remembered for his theory of utilitarianism, in which the morality of actions
is measured by their utility, and for his advocacy of codification as a means of
reform of the law.

15 David Dudley Field (1805-1894) was admitted to practice in New York
in 1828 after an apprenticeship in a law office. In the years after the Civil War
he was a prominent lawyer, argued several landmark cases before the Supreme
Court of the United States, and was elected to the United States House of Representatives to fill a vacancy for a short time. On his role in codification, see the
papers by Pound and Reppy in the *David Dudley Field Centenary Essays* (1949).

16 For an indication of the place of the Field Code in the development of
the law of procedure, see p. 97 *infra*.

and the course of history of the law in the United States would have been significantly altered. As it happened, however, the enthusiasm for codification was on the wane and the movement made little headway from this point. Field's civil code was probably premature. It had been too heroic a task for a single man even of his ability, was not of the highest quality, and was often ignored by the courts of the states in which it was in force. It was the need for unification that was next to give impetus to codification.

The desirability of uniformity among the laws of the states was recognized in 1878 at the time of the organization of the American Bar Association, which included as one of its original objectives the promotion of "uniformity of legislation throughout the Union." In 1889 the Association appointed a Committee on Uniform State Laws and in 1890 the New York legislature authorized the appointment by the governor of commissioners to confer with representatives of other states on the preparation of uniform laws. Under the leadership of the American Bar Association and the State of New York, the National Conference of Commissioners on Uniform State Laws was organized.[17] Its first meeting was held in 1892 and by 1912 all of the states officially participated in the Conference. Each state is represented by commissioners, usually three in number, who are appointed by the governor from the bench, the bar, and the law faculties, to serve without compensation. The Commissioners meet annually for a week to discuss proposed laws, but most of the preliminary work is done in committees which function much as the committees of a legislature. The Conference is, however, not a legislative body and the Commissioners have no power to enact laws or to obligate their respective states to do so. They can only recommend laws to the legislatures of the states, which are free to adopt, with or without amendments, or to reject their proposals. Nevertheless, they have been remarkably successful in furthering the cause of uniformity, particularly in the field of commercial law where the need is perhaps most clear. Uniform acts are promulgated by the Commissioners when they have concluded that uniformity is desirable in the subject in question. Model acts are drafted when there is no special need for uniformity but there is a demand for legislation in a number

---

17 For more on this organization, see Day, *The National Conference of Commissioners on Uniform State Laws*, 8 U. Fla. L. Rev. 276 (1955).

of states. The Commissioners currently recommend sixty-eight uniform and eighteen model acts.[18] Many others which were formerly recommended have been withdrawn for a variety of reasons. Only a few of these, such as the Negotiable Instruments Law, the first law proposed by the Conference, have been adopted by all states. A minority has been adopted by more than half of the states. Many have been adopted by only a handful or less. The Commissioners' most ambitious project has been the Uniform Commercial Code.[19]

The leading institution for reform of the law within a single state is the New York State Law Revision Commission. Its origins go back to 1921 when Judge Benjamin N. Cardozo called for a "Ministry of Justice . . . to watch the law in action, observe the manner of its functioning, and report the changes needed when function is deranged."[20] The utility of such an institution should be manifest. There are occasions when the courts find themselves unable to change a rule of case law even though they recognize it as unsound. They may consider that they are bound by their own precedents and conclude that any change is for the legislature. Or they may be willing to overrule a prior decision but have no opportunity to do so because litigants are discouraged by prior decisions or by the cost of appeal from appealing their cases on the particular point. And there are, to be sure, other occasions on which the courts create or retain unsound rules with less justification. But whatever the reason, unless the matter is one of peculiar importance or considerable notoriety it is likely that the legislature will be too concerned with its regular business to take heed. What is needed is a mediator between the courts and the legislature. To this end the New York legislature in 1934 created the Law Revision Commission as an agency of the legislature to make a continuing study of the decisional and statutory law to discover "defects" and "anachronisms" and to recommend changes to bring the law "into harmony with modern conditions." The commissioners are nine in number, four *ex officio* members of the legislature and five appointed by the governor. The latter are usually drawn from the bar and the law faculties in the state. They are salaried, although not full-time, and have the assistance of a per-

---

[18] *Handbook of the National Conference of Commissioners on Uniform State Laws* 341-43 (1962). The handbook is published annually.

[19] The Code is discussed at p. 134 *infra*.

[20] Cardozo, *A Ministry of Justice*, 35 Harv. L. Rev. 113, 114 (1921).

manent full-time staff in addition to consultants who are retained to study particular problems. The work of the Commission has thus far been confined primarily to specific problems in private substantive law and it has avoided questions of political import. Its studies, recommendations, and drafts of proposed statutes are published in annual volumes. Of 245 proposals made to the legislature for 1934 to 1957, 181 became law. Its contributions have been made in such fields as contracts, torts, real property, restitution, corporations, commercial law, and criminal law.[21] While it has been a disappointment to some that the Commission's work has largely been directed to the remedying of isolated defects rather than to the reorganization and revision of broader areas of the law, it has admirably fulfilled the purposes for which it was conceived and similar institutions have been created in several other states.

SUGGESTED READINGS

A brief discussion of the enactment of federal statutes can be found in Zinn, *How Our Laws Are Made* (1959), a pamphlet. Three books on the federal legislative process are: Galloway, *The Legislative Process in Congress* (1953); Gross, *The Legislative Struggle: A Study in Social Combat* (1953); and Riddick, *The United States Congress: Organization and Procedure* (1949). A report on a study of state legislatures is contained in Zeller, *American State Legislatures* (1954). Information on state legislatures is tabulated biennially in Council of State Governments, *The Book of the States* 1962-63, Section II: Legislatures and Legislation (1962).

---

21 For a summary of the Commission's work during its first two decades, see the symposium on *The New York State Law Revision Commission—The Impact of Twenty Years,* 40 Corn. L. Q. 641 (1955).

Chapter VII

Statutes

The judicial attitude toward legislation has undergone substantial change in the United States during the past century. What is the form of statute law? What are the current techniques of statutory interpretation?

FORM OF STATUTE LAW

An act of Congress or of a state legislature begins with a title ("An act to . . ."), which sets forth the subject of the statute, followed by an enacting clause ("Be it enacted by . . ."), and sometimes by a preamble or purpose clause, stating the reason or policy behind the enactment. Then comes the main body or purview of the statute. It is frequently more detailed than would be the case in many civil law systems, and may contain an extensive list of definitions. The emphasis on detail may be due to a variety of factors: the complexity of the subject matter, to which a pluralistic society, a highly developed economy, and a federal system all contribute; the legislator's desire for specificity born of a fear of restrictive interpretation by the courts; and the lower level of abstraction on which the common law lawyer operates. As a corollary, minor amendments to prevent rigidity are relatively easily made.

Because of the number and the variety of legislatures in the United States, it is no easy task to keep up with the avalanche of current legislation. Congressional enactments are first officially published in the form of slip laws, unbound pamphlets for each act which become available almost immediately after presidental approval. They are also promptly published by several unofficial services. At the end of each session of Congress, those enacted during that session are collected in chronological order in the United States Statutes at Large. Official slip laws are not usually available for state legislation, although in some states the publisher of the permanent edition of state statutes issues advance sheets while the legislature is in session. At the end of the session each state publishes the statutes enacted during that session in its session laws, which are also arranged chronologically.

However, the form in which legislation is ordinarily consulted by the lawyer is a compilation of statutes by subject matter. Compilations generally omit repealed and temporary acts, combine and edit the remaining laws as necessary, and arrange them in classified order. The United States Code is the official compilation of federal statutes under fifty title headings. There are also several unofficial annotations of the Code, of which the United States Code Annotated is the most commonly cited. Similar compilations exist for each state under such designations as codes, compilations, consolidations, general statutes, or revisions of statutes. They generally contain the state constitution as well, but municipal charters, ordinances, and codes are available only in special publications for the particular municipality. The term "code" may be misleading for, with few exceptions, such as the Field codes and the codes of Louisiana, which show the influence of French and Spanish law, these compilations are ordered collections of separately enacted statutes rather than unitary codes enacted as such. Indeed, except to the extent that the compilation has itself been enacted into positive law, the original session laws are in principle the final evidence of the law. A minority of the titles of the United States Code as well as the compilations of some of the states have been enacted. In practice, however, the compilations are used for the sake of convenience, even where they have not been enacted.

It may seem surprising that in the United States it is sometimes more difficult to make a thorough nationwide search of statute law than of case law. There is for legislation no current counterpart of the elaborate system of nationwide classification and indexing which exists for judicial decisions. The Shepard's citator system does cover federal and state legislation in most states and includes constitutions, session laws, compiled statutes, city charters, municipal ordinances, and court rules. But while each state compilation has an index which is adequate for that state, there is no comprehensive current index or digest comparable to the American Digest System.

Rules and regulations of federal administrative agencies and executive orders of the President are published, as issued, in the daily Federal Register, and those which are general, permanent, and currently in force are collected and systematically arranged in the Code of Federal Regulations. There are also unofficial services which publish such materials. Publication of state administrative rules and regulations is less well developed and only a few states have systems which compare with that of the federal government. However, unofficial services in special subjects often collect state as well as federal rules and regulations in a particular field.

Techniques of Interpretation

Although the interpretation of statutes raises some questions which are peculiar to the American legal system, many of the fundamentals are familiar to most legal systems. To begin with, it is axiomatic that as between the court and the legislature, the command of the legislature is supreme except, to be sure, on the point of validity of the statute itself. Case law can be and often is altered by statute but, at least in principle, statutes cannot be altered by court decision. The court's function in dealing with legislation is that of interpretation. As to the nature and limits of this function, however, there is no universal agreement.

On the surface, the simplest approach to interpretation is to look to the common meaning of the words used by the legislature. This approach is sometimes implemented by a durable doctrine known as the "plain meaning rule." Its classical formulation is that where the statute is "clear", "plain", and "unambiguous" on its face, so that taken by itself it is fairly susceptible of only one construction, that construction must be given to it and any inquiry into the purposes, background, or legislative history of the statute is foreclosed. The rigors of this rule have been relaxed by permitting an exception where the result would be "cruel", "monstrous", or "absurd", or sometimes merely "impractical", "unjust", or 'unreasonable." With a growing understanding of the difficulties that attend the use of language to express legal rules, there has come a realization that no statute can be so clearly and accurately drawn as to avoid ambiguity entirely and be applied literally in all situations. The emphasis upon the common meaning of words as the principal or exclusive basis for interpretation, and in particular upon the plain meaning rule, has largely given way to a search for the "intention of the legislature."[1]

Legislative "intention" may be understood either in the specific sense of the understanding of the legislators themselves as to the meaning of the statutory language or in the general sense of the purpose that the legislature sought to achieve by enactment of the statute. In the first sense it is often elusive. The number of legislators is large, even in the state legislatures; virtually all legislatures are divided into two houses which function separately; the average legislator can have only a minimal knowledge of the fine points of a bill, which are not usually discussed on the floor; and the problem before the court may have been unforeseen and even unforeseeable at the time of enactment. Yet in spite of these difficulties, the legislative history not infrequently discloses that at least some responsible legislators considered the point before the court and attributed a meaning to the language in question. Even where this is the case, use of extrinsic aids to show legislative intention has been opposed for practical reasons by critics who maintain that, "Aside from a few offices in the larger cities, the materials of legislative history are not available to the lawyer who can afford neither the cost of acquisition, the cost of housing, or the cost of repeatedly examining the whole congressional history."[2] Nevertheless, courts have frequently used extrinsic aids to establish legislative intention as a guide to statutory interpretation[3] Their weight will depend on how reliable they seem as indications of a general intention of the legislature as a whole. Because of the importance of the committee system, the views of the members of a single committee may, with some justification, be taken as those of the entire legislature. The report of a committee which has considered the bill or a statement on the floor of the legislature by the member of that committee who is in charge of the bill may be particularly persuasive; changes in successive

---

[1] See Jones, *The Plain Meaning Rule and Extrinsic Aids in the Interpretation of Federal Statutes*, 25 Wash. U.L.Q. 2 (1939).

[2] Justice Jackson, concurring, in *Schwegmann Bros. v. Calvert Distillers Corp.*, 341 U. S. 384, 396 (1951).

[3] See Jones, *Extrinsic Aids in the Federal Courts*, 25 Iowa L. Rev. 737 (1940).

drafts of the bill and action on proposed amendments may also be considered; but statements of individual legislators made during floor debate rarely show a common understanding and are likely to be the views of only one man. The use of legislative history as a practical matter is largely confined to the interpretation of federal laws because adequate records are not usually available for state legislatures.

Where the legislative history of the statute is not available or, if available, does not indicate any relevant legislative intention in the sense of "meaning", the court may turn instead to legislative intention in the sense of "purpose". The technique of purpose interpretation was applied in English courts some four centuries ago, and the classical statement of the process involves these steps: examination of the law before enactment of the statute; ascertainment of the "mischief or defect" for which the law did not provide; analysis of the legislative remedy; determination of the reason or purpose of the remedy; and application of the statute so as to "suppress the mischief and advance the remedy."[4] Purpose interpretation does not, therefore, require the use of legislative history and is frequently used in the construction of state statutes where records of legislative history are unavailable. The court may even find a helpful statement of the purpose of enactment set forth in the preamble or purpose clause of the statute itself. However, purpose interpretation is not limited to situations where there is no relevant legislative history and it is no less effective where the purpose of the enactment is derived from one of the extrinsic aids already mentioned, or, for example, from a presidential message describing the need for legislation.

Regardless of which approach to statutory interpretation a court may adopt, it may embellish its opinion with one or more of the innumerable time-honored maxims of statutory construction.[5] Many of these are based on assumptions as to how words are commonly used. Thus there is the maxim *expressio unius est exclusio alterius* — the expression of one thing excludes another; the maxim *noscitur a sociis*—the meaning of a word may be determined by reference to the words associated

---

[4] This is the formulation in *Heydon's Case*, 3 Coke 7a, 76 Eng. Rep. 637 (Court of Exchequer 1584).

[5] For an extensive collection of maxims, statutory and otherwise, see *Bouvier's Law Dictionary and Concise Encyclopedia* (8th ed. 1914) under "maxims."

with it; the *ejusdem generis* rule—where general words follow
an enumeration they are to be read as limited to things of the
same general kind as those specifically mentioned; and the rule
that statutes in *pari materia*, that is, on the same subject, are
to be construed consistently with each other. Others reflect
what are assumed to be broad policies of the law. Among these
are the maxims that statutes, on other than procedural matters,
will not be interpreted as retroactive and that penal statutes
are to be strictly construed in favor of the accused.[6] The authority of maxims is weakened by their very number, their gener-
ality, and their inconsistency. There is a maxim for almost every
purpose and for nearly every maxim an opposite can be found.
For example, when a statute is enacted in an area already governed by case law, the prior law is not entirely eradicated but
subsists to the extent that it is not displaced by the statute. In
fixing the limits of the statute a court may call upon the familiar
rule that such statutes in derogation of the common law are to
be narrowly construed, or it may call upon the equally familiar
rule that such remedial statutes are to be broadly construed.[7]
Nevertheless, maxims cannot be disregarded and may be particularly significant in the interpretation of state statutes where
the lack of adequate records makes it more difficult to show
legislative intention.

Weight of Prior Interpretations

The interpretation of statutes also raises a few questions
that are more peculiar to the American legal system. One of
these concerns the role of precedent. Generally, the doctrine
of precedent applies as fully to cases interpreting statutes as to
other cases. One consequence is that a lower court is bound to
follow the interpretation which a higher court has put upon the
same statutory language and is not free to interpret the statute
directly. Indeed the doctrine of precedent seems to have additional force where a statute is concerned for it is generally said
that American courts feel more constrained by their prior interpretations of statutes than by their decisions on non-statutory grounds. The notion is that the legislature has, by its silence

---

[6] This latter rule has been abrogated or modified by statute in a number of
states. See Hall, *Strict or Liberal Construction of Penal Statutes*, 48 Harv. L.
Rev. 748 (1935).

[7] For a list of conflicting maxims, see Llewellyn, *The Common Law Tradition: Deciding Appeals,* Appendix C (1960).

and inaction in failing to amend the statute, confirmed the prior interpretation even though it may have been erroneous. Quite plainly, this reasoning fails to take account of the many other possible explanations for legislative inaction, but it may be more persuasive where the statute or its relevant language has been reenacted without change following the prior interpretation.

A situation analogous to that of reenactment after court interpretation arises in the case of a "borrowed" statute. In many instances state statutes have been fashioned after or copied outright from those of other states. Usually the statute has been construed by the courts of the state of its origin at the time of its enactment by the borrowing state. What weight should be given to such out-of-state decisions? Although the courts of one state are not bound by the doctrine of precedent to follow out-of-state decisions, the courts of the borrowing state will usually apply the statute as it had been construed by the courts in the state of its origin up to the time that it was borrowed, on the assumption that the legislature intended to introduce not only the statute itself, but the judicial exposition of the statute as well.

Adherence to out-of-state precedent in the interpretation of statutes is of particular significance in the case of uniform laws. Since such statutes are promulgated for the purpose of making uniform the law of the states which adopt them, it is important that their interpretation be uniform. Decisions from other states should therefore be respected even when they came after the date of enactment by the state where the subsequent case has arisen. To implement this policy, each of the uniform acts provides that it shall be interpreted so as "to make uniform the law" among the states which adopt it.

Prior interpretations of a statute by an agency charged with its administration are also given special weight, particularly when adhered to over a period of time. The creation of the agency may have been, at least in part, the result of a need for highly specialized technical knowledge, and the expertise which such a body gains from everyday experience in administering the statute is entitled to respectful consideration, even by the court that reviews its activities.

Judicial Attitude Toward Legislation

The end result of a judicial exercise in statutory construction may depend not only upon which technique of interpretation the court chooses to emphasize, but also upon its attitude toward legislation in general. For, although in principle a statute cannot be altered by judicial decision, in practice it is within the power of the court through interpretation to give free rein to the statute or to hobble it. During much of the nineteenth century the orthodox judicial attitude toward statutes regarded the legislature as encroaching upon the courts in their role of creating, or at least declaring, the common law. Legislation was regarded as exceptional and was applied strictly and narrowly so as to confine it to the cases which it expressly covered. One observer remarked of the English courts in 1882 that some of their rules of statutory interpretation "cannot well be accounted for except upon the theory that Parliament generally changes the law for the worse, and that the business of the judge is to keep the mischief of its interference within the narrowest possible bounds."[8] Fortunately this restrictive attitude no longer prevails in the United States, and it can be expected that a statute will be given a fair and liberal interpretation to cover the entire field that it was intended to cover.[9]

One vestige of the former attitude, however, remains in the reluctance of courts to use statutes as bases of reasoning by analogy. The problem was well stated by Chief Justice Harlan Fiske Stone: "The reception which the courts have accorded to statutes presents a curiously illogical chapter in the history of the common law. Notwithstanding their genius for the generation of new law from that already established, the common-law courts have given little recognition to statutes as starting points for judicial law-making comparable to judicial decisions. They have long recognized the supremacy of statutes over judge-made law, but it has been the supremacy of a command to be obeyed according to its letter, to be treated as otherwise of little consequence. The fact that the command involves recognition of a policy by the supreme lawmaking body has seldom been regarded by courts as significant, either as a social datum or as a point of departure for the process of judicial reasoning by which the common law has expanded. . . . I can find in the history and principles of the common law no adequate reason for our failure to treat a statute much more as we treat a judicial

---

8 Pollock, *Essays in Jurisprudence and Ethics* 85 (1882).
9 See Pound, *Common Law and Legislation,* 21 Harv. L. Rev. 383 (1908).

precedent, as both a declaration and a source of law, and as a premise for legal reasoning."[10]

In spite of their general reluctance to reason by analogy from legislative commands, there are two classes of cases in which courts have derived general principles from statutes and have applied them to cases not within their express terms. One of these involves illegal contracts and the other negligence as a matter of law. Where a statute forbids certain activity, makes it an offense, and provides a penalty, it does not commonly expressly make void a contract the making or performance of which violates its terms, nor does it usually confer a right of recovery upon one who is injured by the failure of another to comply with the statute. Nevertheless, a court will, with some exceptions, refuse to enforce such a contract, thus giving support to the broad legislative policy behind the statute. A court will also, again subject to some exceptions, allow recovery to an injured party upon a showing that the violation of the statute caused the loss, regardless of whether there was actual fault as is usually required in an action based on negligence where no statute is involved. The violation of the statute is said to be negligence as a matter of law. Aside from these two well recognized classes of cases, however, it is unusual for courts to give more than literal scope to the commands of the legislature and to reason by analogy from a statute.[11]

SUGGESTED READINGS

An interesting history of the background and interpretation of a single statute is set out in Levi, *An Introduction to Legal Reasoning* (1962). For a thought-provoking discussion by a judge on the role of the court in dealing with legislation, see Breitel, *The Courts and Lawmaking* in *Legal Institutions Today and Tomorrow* (Paulsen, editor 1959). There is a good

---

[10] Stone, *The Common Law in the United States*, 50 Harv. L. Rev. 4, 12-13 (1936).

[11] There have been, to be sure, some notable exceptions. For example the Uniform Sales Act allows recovery by the buyer against the seller for breach of warranty (without any proof of fault) in the case of the sale of goods. In *Hoisting Engine Sales Co. v. Hart*, 237 N. Y. 30, 142 N. E. 342 (1923), the court found a warranty in the lease of a derrick, on the ground that the transaction was analogous to a sale. However, in *Perlmutter v. Beth David Hospital*, 308 N. Y. 100, 123 N. E. 2d 792 (1954), the same court refused to find a warranty in the case of a blood transfusion because the transaction was not a sale. The possibility of reasoning by analogy was not discussed.

discussion on sources of law in Patterson, *Jurisprudence: Men and Ideas of the Law*, Chapter 9 (1953), an introductory work on legal philosophy. The best starting point for a practical exercise in statutory interpretation is Dowling, Patterson, and Powell, *Materials for Legal Method* (2nd ed. by Jones 1952), an introductory casebook. Another casebook with many useful notes and other materials on legislation is Read, MacDonald, and Fordham, *Cases and Other Materials on Legislation* (1959). A standard treatise on interpretation of statutes is Sutherland, *Statutes and Statutory Construction* (3rd ed. by Horack 1943) in three volumes with current pocket supplements.

Chapter VIII

Secondary Authority

The common law is sometimes supposed to hold "secondary authority", such as treatises, legal periodicals, and encyclopedias, in low esteem. How available and how influential are such materials in the United States? What has been the impact of the Restatement of the Law?

SIGNIFICANCE OF SECONDARY AUTHORITY

"Secondary authority" is a general term which embraces treatises, legal periodicals, encyclopedias, and other aids to finding and interpreting such "primary authority" as statutes and cases. Such a work may be useful for its collection of citations, for its organization of the subject matter, for its statement of legal rules, or for its original analysis, criticism, and proposals for improvement. The quality and reliability of secondary authorities varies widely. Although practitioners' writings are not lacking, most of the significant works have emanated from the law faculties.

Secondary authorities are, at most, persuasive. No judge is bound to follow the views of an author in the way that he may be bound to follow a statute or a case. Practically, however, secondary authority is frequently cited by judges in their opinions, and there are some notable instances in which scholars have led the way for the courts to follow: a law review article by two young men on the right of privacy helped to persuade many courts to recognize that right;[1] and one by a distinguished legal historian on the history of the Judiciary Act of 1789 was relied

---

[1] Brandeis and Warren, *The Right of Privacy*, 4 Harv. L. Rev. 193 (1890). Twenty-six years later Brandeis became a member of the Supreme Court of the United States.

[2] Warren, *New Light on the History of the Federal Judiciary Act of 1789*, 37 Harv. L. Rev. 49 (1923), cited in *Erie Railroad Co.* v. *Tompkins*, 304 U. S. 64, 72-73 (1938).

upon by the Supreme Court of the United States in overruling *Swift* v. *Tyson* in the case of *Erie Railroad Co.* v. *Tompkins*.[2] However, the effect of secondary authority depends more upon its intrinsic worth and upon the court's esteem for the particular writer than upon any veneration of scholars in general.

The volume of systematic commentary on the law by distinguished authors is not as great as might be expected in view of the large number of lawyers and of university law schools in the United States. The legal encyclopedias are not the work of scholars and their value lies more in their accessibility than in the quality of their distillations of the law. While there have been some multi-volume American treatises of the highest quality, such as Corbin on *Contracts*, Powell on *Real Property*, Scott on *Trusts*, Wigmore on *Evidence*, and Williston on *Contracts*, there are many fields of law, including constitutional law, commercial law, and family law, for which there is no comparable work. One reason for the scarcity of systematic exegesis is the inherent difficulty of preparing comprehensive treatises in a system that has the dual characteristics of federalism and the common law. Treatises typically contain statements of minority as well as majority rules, supported by extensive citations of cases and statutes culled from the courts of the fifty states and from the federal courts. The prospect of collecting such authority may be less than attractive to the mature and reflective scholar. A second reason is that much of the effort which might otherwise go into treatises goes into alternative lines of scholarly endeavor, notably casebooks and articles in legal periodicals. Whereas formerly the professor's lecture notes could serve as the germ of later published treatises, the advent of the case method put an end to the preparation of formal lectures and the energies of the leading faculties were turned instead to the preparation of casebooks for student use. The introduction of the university law reviews near the turn of the century provided yet another alternative to the writing of treatises, and since that time much of the original thought about law in the United States has found expression in these journals, where it is not uncommon for a single article covering a substantial topic to be as long as fifty or one hundred pages.[3] Nevertheless, there

---

[3] Comment on individual cases is left, by and large, to the student editors of the reviews. It should be remembered that the judge's discussion of principles is often extensive, so that need for commentary is less acute than in countries where opinions are more laconic.

can be found in the United States most of the varieties of legal writing which are available elsewhere, along with a few which are indigenous.

Kinds of Secondary Authority

The principal kinds of secondary authority are these:

(1) *Dictionaries.* The traditional American law dictionary is *Bouvier's Law Dictionary and Concise Encyclopedia* (8th ed. by Rawle 1914), in three volumes. A popular one volume work is *Black's Law Dictionary* (4th ed. 1951). The statements of law sometimes appended to the definitions contained in these sources should not, however, be taken as reliable.

(2) *Encyclopedias.* There are two popular general encyclopedias, *American Jurisprudence* in 58 volumes, now in the process of revision as *American Jurisprudence 2d,* and *Corpus Juris Secundum* in 101 volumes. Both are well indexed, contain ample citations, and are kept up to date with annual cumulative supplements to each volume. They are concerned mainly with the exposition of the law as it is rather than with critical analysis, and are superficial and less reliable than the better treatises and texts. The contributions, which are unsigned, are those of the publisher's permanent staff rather than of known scholars.

(3) *Treatises and text books.* Treatises and text books may be designed to serve several purposes. Some treatises, like those of Corbin, Powell, Scott, Wigmore, and Williston, mentioned above, are carefully reasoned and scholarly expositions of a field with explanation of the reasons behind the rules and criticism of the present state of the law. They are equally useful to the scholar and the practitioner. Others, often written by practicing lawyers on specialized topics such as automobile accidents or insurance, are intended primarily for the practitioner whose chief concern is with the present state of the law and who is searching for a case or other authority in a particular field. Treatises of both kinds are usually kept up to date with annual cumulative supplements. Single-volume textbooks, such as Prosser, *Handbook of the Law of Torts* (2nd ed. 1955) or Gilmore and Black, *The Law of Admiralty* (1957), have been written in many fields to serve as introductory works for students as well as practitioners. Occasionally shorter student editions of major treatises, such as those of Corbin and Williston,

have been published. In addition there are many excellent monographs on particular aspects of the law, such as Freund, *The Supreme Court of the United States: Its Business, Purposes, and Performance* (1961) and Gellhorn, *American Rights: The Constitution in Action* (1960).

(4) *Casebooks.* While the casebook is chiefly a teaching tool for student use, it should not be ignored as a research work as well. Many casebooks, such as Baker and Cary, *Cases and Materials on Corporations* (1959) and Patterson, Goble, and Jones, *Cases and Materials on Contracts* (1957), contain copious notes and references to leading articles as well as cases. Since they are more frequently revised than many text books, they may contain more recent material.

(5) *Legal periodicals.* The most distinguished American legal periodicals are the university law reviews, which now number nearly one hundred. Traditionally they are edited by top-ranking students and print student notes and comments as well as signed leading articles and book reviews by professors, lawyers, and judges. The leading articles are apt to be more original, argumentative, and critical than is the material found in treatises. The quality of the student work is often high and has not infrequently merited citation by the courts. Many reviews stress the local law of their jurisdiction or geographical area. A few emphasize special fields, for example the *Tulane Law Review* is devoted to the civil law, comparative law, and codification. Aside from the university law reviews, there are many journals that are published by bar associations and specialized groups. Examples are the *American Bar Association Journal*, the *Journal of Legal Education*, the *American Journal of International Law*, and the *American Journal of Comparative Law*. A summary of recent developments in various fields is published each year in the *Annual Survey of American Law* of the New York University School of Law. Work published in most English language periodicals in the United States and elsewhere is indexed in the comprehensive and cumulative *Index to Legal Periodicals*, and a selected list of books and articles is published each year by the Harvard Law School Library in its *Annual Legal Bibliography*.

(6) *Loose-leaf services.* Loose-leaf services, notably those of the Commerce Clearing House (CCH) and Prentice-Hall, enable the lawyer to keep current in such rapidly changing fields as federal and state taxation, business regulation, and

adminstrative law. Examples are the CCH *Standard Federal Tax Reporter* and the Prentice-Hall *Corporation Guide.* Each service covers one specific field as completely as possible, including all types of authority together with comment and explanations.

(7) *Miscellaneous.* The lawyer who is concerned with the drafting of legal documents may find help in numerous form books, some general and some specialized, which collect standard forms for such documents, both substantive and procedural. Another useful aid for the practitioner is the *Martindale-Hubbell Law Directory,* a four volume set which contains a directory of American lawyers and a collection of brief digests of the law of the fifty states and many foreign countries.

Restatement of the Law

No discussion of secondary authority in the United States would be complete without mention of that unique effort at systematization of case law which culminated in the Restatement of the Law.[4] When the American Law Institute was organized in 1923, its objectives included "the clarification and simplification of the law." Its founders had concluded that, "Two chief defects in American law are its uncertainty and its complexity. These defects cause useless litigation, prevent resort to the courts to enforce just rights, make it often impossible to advise persons of their rights, and when litigation is begun, create delay and expense." They saw in the growing number of decisions a threat to the vitality of the law. It was becoming increasingly difficult for the lawyer working on a case to find, read, and digest the relevant cases of the courts in his own state and when this task yielded up no firm precedent, he was thrown upon the almost inexhaustible store of cases decided in the courts of other states and in the federal courts. They concluded that what was needed in those areas of the law that had not submitted to legislation was an authority greater than that of any single treatise to bring order into the chaos of case law.

To meet this need the Restatement was prepared under

---

[4] On the Restatement generally, see Lewis, "History of the Restatement," contained in *Restatement in the Courts* 1 (perm. ed. 1945); Goodrich, *The Story of the American Law Institute,* 1951 Wash. U. L. Q. 283 (1951); Clark, *The Restatement of the Law of Contracts,* 42 Yale L. J. 643 (1933).

the auspices of the Institute. It covers nine fields in which case law was dominant and the effect of varying state statutes was minimal: agency, conflict of laws, contracts, judgments, property, restitution, security, torts, and trusts. The Restatement in each field was drafted by a reporter, who was an eminent law teacher, in collaboration with a group of advisors, including teachers, practitioners, and judges. The results of their combined efforts were then considered and approved by the Council of the Institute and finally by the membership of the Institute. The Restatement of Property, the most voluminous, contains 568 sections, fills four volumes, digests 30,000 cases, took seventeen years to prepare, and occupied the time of scholars from seven different law faculties. The complete Restatement of the Law took two decades to complete and, with index and special materials, comes to twenty volumes plus annotations for many states. The Restatement of each field is divided into sections, which are black-letter statements of principles or rules, often with subdivisions. Most sections are followed by comments, which explain their purpose and scope, and by illustrations of their application. Cases are not commonly cited, nor are conflicting views discussed.

Although the Restatement is intended to be what its name signifies, it is not merely a summary of what has been decided by the courts in the past; on occasions it has adopted a minority rule on the ground that it is demonstrably better than the majority rule. But neither is the Restatement a statement of what the Institute would like to see the law become in the future. Rather it is the considered opinion of some of the country's foremost legal scholars as to the law which would be applied by an enlightened court today. The quality and significance of the Restatement is not the same in all of its fields. On the whole its influence has been considerably greater than that of an ordinary treatise, but it is by no means followed as a code. From 1923 to 1950 the Restatement was cited a total of nearly 18,000 times by appellate courts, and citations continue at a rate of about 1,200 a year. These have been collected in the volumes entitled *Restatement in the Courts*. It has been claimed by its sponsors that in fewer than two percent of the cases has there been disagreement with the principles of the Restatement, but even assuming that the figure is accurate, it is difficult to estimate the importance of this minority of cases. In many states there is said to be no firm precedent on roughly one half of the points covered by the Restatement, which suggests that it can exercise an important influence toward unification when a new question arises. The Restatement has not, however, resulted in a movement for codification. Amendments have occasionally been made where required by changing case law, and a second edition, called the Restatement Second, has been prepared or is in the process of preparation in several fields.[5] But it was never the intention of its sponsors to aim at codification, and the Restatement is designed to preserve, not to alter, the common law practice of expressing and adapting law to social change.

Suggested Readings

The most comprehensive manual for legal research is Price and Bitner, *Effective Legal Research* (1953), also available in a revised student edition (1962). Pollack, *Fundamentals of Legal Research* (2nd ed. 1962) is a similar work.

---

[5] The Restatement Second has been completed and published for Agency (1958) and for Trusts (1959); drafts have been published for Conflict of Laws and for Torts and for a new Restatement of the Foreign Relations Law of the United States; and an advisory committee has been established for Contracts.

Part Two

Organization and Substance

Chapter IX

Classification

Several factors make the classification of American law particularly difficult. Fundamental distinctions can, however, be drawn between law and equity, between substance and procedure, and between public and private law. What are these distinctions and how useful are they in the characterization of legal problems?

THE PROBLEM OF CLASSIFICATION

Any system of law can be divided into categories according to a more or less rational scheme of classification. The lawyer, perhaps unconsciously, makes a preliminary characterization of a problem as a means of orientation and an essential prelude to analysis and research. Characterization may also have legal consequences as where, for example, it determines the choice of law rule which a court will apply. Yet no system of classification can avoid arbitrariness and ambiguity and several features of American law make classification particularly difficult. First, it has no comprehensive plan of codification from which to derive a scheme of classification. Second, its case-oriented approach is more pragmatic and empirical than theoretical and abstract and does not lend itself to generalization. It is symptomatic that the American lawyer does not see the broad general categories that are perceived by his counterparts in civil law countries.[1] Third, the common methods and techniques which pervade all branches of law tend to inhibit the development of autonomous fields.

---

[1] The fragmentation of American law is most acute in the field of private law, where it was encouraged by the multifarious forms of action in the law courts before the procedural reforms of the nineteenth century. Thus the area of private law known in civil law countries as "civil law" is thought of by the American lawyer as such separate subjects as contracts, torts, property, and family law, and the field of torts, for example, is divided into such distinct torts as assault, battery, and trespass. See p. 124 *infra*.

This is due in part to the absence of special courts, like those found in some civil law countries, for such major branches as public and commercial law.

In spite of these difficulties, there are some well recognized distinctions which are useful for the purposes of orientation, analysis, and research, and which are perpetuated through the content of law school courses and casebooks, through the titles of treatises and the Restatement, through the topic headings of digests and encyclopedias, and in some instances through the purview of statutes. Three broad divisions will first be considered: that between law and equity, that between substance and procedure, and that between public and private law.

Law and Equity

The history of the distinction between law and equity begins in the developing system of law which followed the Norman conquest of England. A plaintiff who wished to have his complaint heard in the king's courts rather than the local courts had to purchase from the office of the chancellor a writ, or royal command, which fitted the facts of his case and which required the defendant to appear in court. The variety of writs available, and with it the jurisdiction of the king's courts, expanded until the second half of the thirteenth century when, under pressure from the nobility, the power to issue writs was circumscribed, the jurisdiction of the king's courts was limited, and the flexibility of the law was diminished. Nevertheless, there was a residual power in the king and his council to do justice in special cases and he began to refer petitions for redress to the chancellor who, as the chief law member of the council, might give relief as a matter of "grace" or of "conscience" in cases where relief at law was inadequate.

From these beginnings there grew up for non-criminal cases a supplementary system, known as "equity," in which, by the early fifteenth centry, justice was administered through a separate court, the Court of Chancery. The law courts were forced to accept this system after a notorious struggle that ended in the early seventeenth century. Among the distinctive features of a suit in equity as opposed to an action at law were the absence of a jury, a more flexible procedure, and a wider scope of review on appeal. While the law courts were generally restricted to the award of money damages as relief, equity operated on the person of the defendant and the court could, for example, issue an injunction, forbidding him to do specified acts in order to prevent further injury, or it could decree specific performance, ordering him to perform an obligation. If the defendant disobeyed, it could punish him by fine or imprisonment for contempt of court until he complied. But because these equitable remedies were considered to be extraordinary, they were only available where the remedy at law could be shown to be inadequate, and money damages remained the standard kind of relief.[2]

Equity also came to differ from law in substance as well as procedure, as may be seen from one of its most important creations, the trust. The trust concept grew out of the conveyance of property by the owner, now called the settlor, to a transferee, now called the trustee, who was to hold it for the benefit of another, now called the beneficiary. For the transaction to succeed, some means had to be found to compel the trustee to comply with the terms of the trust. Since equity acted upon the person, it was able to enforce the trustee's fiduciary duties by its sanctions of fine and imprisonment while at the same time recognizing the legal ownership of the trustee. Out of the beneficiary's equitable rights came the concept of equitable, as distinguished from legal, ownership. Around this new institution a whole new branch of substantive law was to grow. Today the express trust is widely used in the United States for both real and personal property, especially income-producing securities, and trust administration is fast becoming a task for professionals with the resultant rise of corporate trustees; private express trusts are relied upon to dispose of most substantial family wealth at death; charitable express trusts are used to create large philanthropic foundations. The trust concept has also proved a useful tool in the hands of the courts: resulting trusts, inferred from the circumstances, are used to carry out the presumed intentions of parties to transactions in property;[3] and constructive trusts, im-

---

[2] A claim for breach of an obligation to pay money was an obvious example of a case in which the remedy at law was adequate, but money damages were also held to be "adequate" in most cases of breach of an obligation to deliver goods as well since it was supposed that the obligee could purchase equivalent goods with the sum awarded. Specific performance was allowed, however, for breach of an obligation to convey land, since each piece of land was regarded as unique.

[3] For example: "A deposits money in a bank in the name of B. In the absence of evidence of a different intention on the part of A, B holds his claim against the bank for the amount of the deposit upon a resulting trust for A." *Restatement of Trusts,* Section §440, illustration 2.

plied as a matter of law, have become an essential device for avoiding unjust enrichment in cases of fraud and mistake.[4]

Equity found its way into most of the colonies in spite of some resistence which stemmed from the close relationship which equity had had to the crown. It was generally received in the states, was developed by the courts in the early part of the nineteenth century, and was the subject of one of Story's great treatises. Some states had separate systems of courts for law and equity; others had a single system in which a court might sit as either a law court or an equity court, depending on the nature of the case. Both schemes occasioned inconvenience, expense, and delay, as where a party sought relief in the wrong kind of court and had to begin all over again, and by the middle of the century there was a demand for merger of law and equity. New York led the reform by enactment of the Field Code of Civil Procedure in 1848. It abolished the distinction between a suit in equity and an action at law, substituted a single civil action for the different forms of action previously available, and consolidated the rules of procedure, borrowing heavily from the more liberal equity rules. Law and equity procedure was united in the federal courts as recently as 1938 and has been merged in practically all of the states.

The merger cannot be fully realized, however, because the right to a jury trial under federal and state constitutions generally extends only to cases formerly triable at law and not to those formerly triable in equity, so that for historical reasons the distinction between law and equity must even now be observed for this purpose. Where there are both legal and equitable issues in a jury trial, the legal issues of fact are decided by the jury while the equitable issues are decided by the judge. Moreover, rights which originated in the equity courts are still referred to as "equitable" and are exercised in much the same way and are subject to most of the same limitations as they were in the courts of equity. The most important restriction is that they are still available only where the "legal" remedy is "inadequate."

It is therefore important to realize that "equity" is not a synonym for "general fairness" or "natural justice," but refers to

---

[4] For example: "A, the owner of land, makes a gratuitous conveyance to B. By a mistake in the description in the deed, A transfers not only the tract which he intended to convey but also a second tract which he did not intend to include. B does not know of the mistake and believes that A intended to transfer both tracts. B holds the second tract upon a constructive trust for A." *Restatement of Resolution* §163, illustration 1.

a particular body of rules that originated in a special system of courts. However, these rules have to a considerable extent been assimilated into the appropriate categories of law and are now often regarded as part, for example, of property or contract law. One result has been that most of the leading law schools no longer give a separate course in equity. It is true in the United States, as in England, that "if we were to inquire what it is that all these rules have in common and what it is that marks them off from all other rules administered by our courts, we should by way of answer find nothing but this, that these rules were until lately administered, and administered only, by our courts of equity."[3] Certainly for present purposes, the distinction between law and equity is not a helpful basis for classification.

SUBSTANCE AND PROCEDURE

The distinction between substance and procedure is a more fruitful one. Some such distinction is familiar to all legal systems. In the United States the subject of procedure, or adjective law as it is occasionally called, has taken on special importance not only because of the creative role accorded the courts in all common law countries, but also because of such indigenous factors as the professional emphasis of law study and the complexities of the federal system. The distinction may be important for a variety of purposes: if a statute concerns a matter of "procedure" rather than "substance" it will be unaffected by constitutional prohibitions against retroactive legislation; if a question is one of "procedure" rather than "substance" a federal court in a diversity case will follow federal law rather than defer to state law under *Erie Railroad Co.* v. *Tompkins;*[4] if an issue is one of "procedure" rather than "substance" a state court will apply its own law rather than the law of some other state whose law would be chosen to govern the chief rights and liabilities.

The line of demarcation is sometimes difficult to fix and what a court will consider to be "substance" and what "procedure" in a particular case may depend upon the purpose for which the distinction is to be drawn. Thus a statute of limitations may be regarded as "procedural," as barring a remedy, for one purpose and as "substantive," as terminating a right, for another. Nevertheless, the number of borderline cases is rela-

---

[3] Maitland, *Lectures on Equity* 1-2 (1909), speaking of equity in England.
[4] See p. 42 *supra*.

tively small, and the boundaries of the field of procedure are in the main well established. It is concerned with all aspects of the conduct of legal controversy before the courts, including access to the courts, who may sue and be sued, the form of the action, the availability of countervailing claims, the conditions of maintaining suit, the steps before trial, the method of proof, the effects of the court's judgment, remedies, and appeals.

Procedure includes both criminal and civil procedure. It also encompasses the subject of evidence, which is concerned with the rules relating to proof before a court. Because the significance and intricacy of this field is greatly heightened by the adversary system and the use of the jury, the law of evidence is often treated as a distinct branch of the law. Finally, the subject of conflict of laws has a very heavy procedural ingredient and, for the sake of convenience, is placed here under the heading of procedure.[5]

Public and Private Law

The division of substantive law into public and private law is, while not uncommon, of more questionable utility than the division of law into substance and procedure.[6] As the Supreme Court of the United States has said, "It is often convenient to describe particular claims as invoking public or private rights, and this handy classification is doubtless valid for some purposes. But usually the real significance and legal consequence of each term will depend upon its context and the nature of the interests it is invoked to distinguish."[7]

Because there is no special system of courts to handle public law matters, there is rarely an occasion when the distinction is of practical importance. It his been suggested that public law encompasses those rights which are enforced through the administrative process while private law is concerned with those which are left to enforcement on private intiative through the law courts.[8] This, however, gives but a narrow compass to public

---

[5] The subject of federal jurisdiction, which is concerned with the jurisdiction of the federal courts, is also essentially procedural. It has been discussed in an earlier chapter and will not be repeated here.

[6] The distinction between public and private law should not be confused with that between public and private laws, or enactments. See fn. 9, p. 62 *supra.*

[7] Justice Jackson in *Garner* v. *Teamsters Union,* 346 U.S. 485, 494 (1953).

[8] *Ibid.*

law, for even constitutional law, for example, is part of the everyday work of the ordinary courts in resolving suits between private parties. Perhaps the lawyer tends to think of public law, if he concerns himself with the distinction at all, in the classic sense of a branch of law devoted to the functioning of government and the adjustment of relations between individuals and the government, while private law is occupied with the rights of individuals among themselves. Of course even this distinction is difficult to apply to the increasing number of situations where the state intervenes or becomes involved in relations between private individuals.

Whatever the merits or nature of the distinction, all lawyers would probably include in public law the fields of constitutional law and administrative law. Also included are labor law, which is primarily concerned with government control over labor relations, and trade regulation, which is primarily concerned with government control over business activity, as well as criminal law, which directly affects the relationship between the individual and the government. The inclusion of tax law may be more controversial because of its strong affinity in practice with private law fields such as corporation and property law.[9] Private law is more fragmented. What is known in most civil law countries as "civil law," is broken down into contracts, family law, property law, and torts. The law of negotiable instruments, sales, and secured transactions are only now being recognized as parts of a whole called commercial law. And the subjects of agency, corporations, and partnerships can only with some artifice be grouped for the sake of convenience under the heading of business enterprises.[10]

SUGGESTED READINGS

There is no general work on classification in American law. Even the subject of equity, as such, has had little recent attention from scholarly writers. A standard introductory volume is

---

[9] The field of international law, by which is meant public international law, is somewhat a branch unto itself and is not discussed here because its substance is less peculiar than that of the other fields to the United States.

[10] Other fields, such as admiralty or maritime law, bankruptcy, copyrights, insurance, patents, and trusts, are discussed under the most appropriate of the topics named. A few, such as comparative law, and jurisprudence (as legal philosophy is frequently called), are not sufficiently indigenous to warrant discussion.

McClintock, *Handbook of the Principles of Equity* (2nd ed. 1948). An older book is Walsh, *A Treatise on Equity* (1930). The newest work is de Funiak, *Handbook of Modern Equity* (2nd ed. 1956). There is also a five-volume treatise, Pomeroy, *A Treatise on Equity Jurisprudence* (5th ed. by Symons 1941). Substantive aspects of the field, such as trusts, may be found in the works cited under the appropriate fields of law. Some of the more important areas of American law are discussed briefly in Berman (editor), *Talks on American Law* (1961), a series of radio broadcasts to foreign audiences, and in Gavit, *Introduction to the Study of Law* (1951).

Chapter X

Procedure

The subjects of civil procedure, criminal procedure, evidence, and conflict of laws may be grouped under the general heading of procedure. What factors have influenced their development and contributed to their distinctive characteristics? How is litigation carried on in the United States?

CIVIL PROCEDURE

SCOPE AND SOURCES

Procedure in the United States has been greatly influenced by two factors. First, the adversary rather than inquisitorial character of litigation has encouraged the opposing lawyers to act as zealous partisans in presenting their cases, has contributed to a tradition of surprise and proprietorship over witnesses and information, and has accorded a relatively passive role to the judge, who acts only as arbiter and undertakes no independent investigation. Second, the institution of the jury has tended to compress the trial, has given it a dramatic flavor, and has resulted in elaborate rules to separate the functions of the jury from those of the judge and to control the jury. In spite of these similarities in approach to procedural problems, each state court system, as well as the federal court system, operates under its own law of civil procedure.

At first the states adapted their procedural law from that of England, which was compounded of court rules, judicial decisions, custom, and occasional statutes, but dissatisfaction with its rigidity and formality led reformers to seek more extensive legislation. The contributions of the Field Code, enacted in New

York in 1848, have already been mentioned,[1] and as other states followed the lead of New York in enacting procedural codes, control over procedure passed to the legislatures. But the codes themselves proved rigid and became increasingly detailed,[2] and pressure built up to return the rule-making function to the courts. In 1934 Congress was persuaded to give the Supreme Court of the United States the power to make general rules of procedure for the district courts, subject to congressional disapproval. Complete or substantial rule-making power has also been given to the courts in a growing number of states, where it is usually exercised by the highest state court with the assistance of an advisory body such as a judicial council. In 1938 the Supreme Court promulgated the Federal Rules of Civil Procedure, which had been prepared by an Advisory Committee drawn from the bench and bar. The Rules have since been amended and are under continuous study by the Judicial Conference of the United States, a group of senior federal judges which is advised by committees of judges, lawyers, and professors. They embody many of the most modern ideas on procedure and are not only law for the federal district courts but have been closely copied in over half of the states. Nevertheless, the law of civil procedure is far from uniform.

Procedure varies not only with the jurisdiction but also with the remedy sought by the plaintiff. Most civil actions involve claims for compensatory money damages; more than half of the civil actions filed in the major trial courts of the country involve damage claims for personal injury.[3] In a few instances remedies at law were specific rather than compensatory: replevin was available to compel the return of personal property which had been wrongfully taken, and ejectment to recover possession of real property. These names are still in common use even where there is now only one form of civil action. But aside from these exceptional cases, money damages are the standard remedy unless it is shown that compensatory relief will be inadequate so that equitable relief, such as a decree of specific performance or an injunction, may be granted. The following discussion is of necessity both general and simplified and is limited to the

---

[1] See p. 66 *supra*.

[2] In New York the successor to the Field Code at one time contained upwards of three thousand sections.

[3] A substantial portion of the remainder are family disputes. While business disputes play numerically a minor role, they attract much of the attention of the profession.

most common sort of case, an action *in personam,* a personal
action against the defendant, for compensatory money damages.[4] The object of such an action is to determine the rights of
the parties with respect to the controversy and to impose liability. An action may also be one *in rem,* in which the purpose
is not to impose liability upon anyone, but to affect the interests
of all persons in a thing. Or an action may be one *quasi in rem,*
to affect the interests of particular persons in a thing. In addition, the federal courts and the courts of most states are now
permitted under special statutes to grant declaratory judgments,
declaring the rights between the parties, where there is an actual controversy between adversary parties but where other relief would be premature, unnecessary, or ineffective.[5]

CHARACTERISTICS — BEFORE TRIAL

There is a sharp distinction between the proceedings which
precede the trial and the trial itself. At the trial the issues of
fact will be heard and determined. In the pre-trial proceedings
these issues must be defined and the adversaries must be given
adequate notice to prevent their surprise at the trial. This is of
special importance because the trial, owing to the influence of
the jury system, is normally concentrated in one continuous
hearing in open court. Any rulings before trial are made, usually after argument, by a judge without a jury.

Parties to litigation are almost invariably represented by
lawyers, who undertake the preparation of the necessary papers
and appear in court. The steps taken by the parties in the description which follows are, therefore, ordinarily taken by their
lawyers in their clients' behalf.

An action is commenced by two writings, a complaint and
a summons. The complaint is a statement which sets out the
nature of the plaintiff's claim and his demand for relief. The
summons is a notice informing the defendant that an action

---

4 Claims by the defendant against the plaintiff and claims by or against third
parties will not be discussed here. The discussion assumes that only two parties
are involved.

5 There are special procedures for the prerogative writs of certiorari, habeas
corpus, mandamus, prohibition, and quo warranto, for summary proceedings,
and for some courts of limited jurisdiction. A writ of habeas corpus, for example,
is available under proper circumstances to a person who has been physically detained by another, whether in a public or private capacity, and directs the person
detaining him to produce "the body" of the detained person in court for a
determination of the legality of the detention.

is being brought against him and calling upon him to answer the complaint. In order to meet the constitutional requirement of due process, service of the summons must be by a means which is reasonably designed to give the defendant notice. Ordinarily it is delivered to him personally or left with an appropriate person at his residence or place of business within the geographical jurisdiction of the court. In special cases service may be accomplished by mail, by publication, or by some other means. The defendant then commonly enters an appearance by filing a paper, known as an answer, which is responsive to the complaint; if he does not appear, a default judgment may be entered against him. The plaintiff's complaint, the defendant's answer, and any reply which the plaintiff may file, comprise the pleadings.[6] In a proper case the plaintiff may also avail himself of provisional remedies to ensure that his action, if successful, will not have been futile. For example, he may be able through an attachment to have the defendant's property seized and held as security for any judgment, or to obtain a temporary injunction or restraining order to prevent the defendant from taking action to frustrate the plaintiff's suit.

Before the enactment of the procedural codes, the theory of pleading, known as common law pleading, was that the parties themselves should develop a single precise issue of fact or of law by means of elaborate written pleadings exchanged in advance of trial. One of the innovations of the Field Code was to replace this "issue pleading" with "fact pleading," in which the parties were asked only to plead simple statements of the essential facts which they expected to prove at the trial. But there was confusion over the particularity with which facts should be stated, and the Federal Rules of Civil Procedure abandoned "fact pleading" in favor of what has sometimes been called "notice pleading." Under the Rules the emphasis is less on pleadings than on other more efficient means of obtaining information. The complaint need contain only a short and plain statement of the claim showing that the plaintiff is entitled to relief; allegations may be general and even inconsistent; and protection against surprise at trial is afforded by important new

---

[6] In the United States the term "pleading" in civil procedure is limited to the exchange of these written documents before trial and does not include, for example, the lawyer's argument at the trial.

pre-trial procedures.[7] The opportunities to learn about an opponent's case include, for example, the right to interrogate the other party, to take the deposition of any person, and to inspect documents and property. In addition, the judge may call a pre-trial conference, a hearing at which both sides are present, in order to limit the issues and obtain admissions which will avoid unnecessary proof. Important by-products of the pre-trial conference are said to be the settlement of many cases without trial and the shortening of trials through concessions, limitation of issues, and better preparation.

Pre-trial procedure will occasionally result in a decision by the court that there should be no trial at all. The defendant may attack the legal basis of the plaintiff's case by a motion[8] to dismiss the complaint on the ground that it fails to state a legally sufficient cause of action or claim for relief. This is known in some states as a demurrer. The judge will grant the defendant's motion only if, on the assumption that all of the allegations of the complaint were true, the plaintiff would still have no right to relief. Such motions, however, rarely end the litigation. If the complaint is found to be insufficient, the plaintiff will ordinarily be allowed to amend it; if it is found to be sufficient, the defendant will usually interpose an answer which raises an issue of fact. This the defendant may do in two ways, either by denying some or all of the plaintiff's allegations or by alleging additional facts which constitute a defense. Under modern pre-trial procedure, however, it is sometimes possible to resolve even an issue of fact before trial. The judge may grant a

---

[7] For example, the Complaint for Negligence, as found in Form 9 of the Federal Rules of Civil Procedure, reads:

1. Allegation of jurisdiction.

2. On June 1, 1936, in a public highway called Boylston Street in Boston, Massachusetts, defendant negligently drove a motor vehicle against plaintiff who was then crossing said highway.

3. As a result plaintiff was thrown down and had his leg broken and was otherwise injured, was prevented from transacting his business, suffered great pain of body and mind, and incurred expenses for medical attention and hospitalization in the sum of one thousand dollars.

Wherefore plaintiff demands judgment against defendant in the sum of ten thousand dollars and costs.

Under "fact pleading" the complaint would be more detailed and contain more paragraphs.

[8] A motion is an application to the court for a ruling, in this case an order to dismiss. An order is the traditional form for any judicial determination, short of a final judgment disposing of the entire case.

motion for summary judgment in favor of either party if he determines, on the basis of affidavits and other documents that there is no genuine issue of fact justifying a trial. The defendant may also make a variety of motions which do not go to the merits of the controversy and which range from a motion to dismiss the complaint because the court does not have jurisdiction, to a motion to require the plaintiff to make his complaint more definite and certain or to give further particulars on some matter.

If the plaintiff's complaint has withstood the defensive tactics of his adversary and if the case is not one of the great majority which are settled before trial, the plaintiff will request the clerk of the court to put the case on a list, called a calendar or docket, to await trial. Because of the number of litigants who precede him, he may have to wait for a substantial period of time, well over a year in some congested courts, before his case comes to trial.

Characteristics — Trial

Although modern pre-trial procedure has done much to counter the tradition of surprise and proprietorship over proof, it is still a basic tenet that each party can most effectively present his own case and, after it has been subjected to attack by his adversary, the truth can then be determined by an impartial tribunal. The trial is held before a single judge, who may sit with or without a jury.[9] It may last for a matter of hours, days, or even weeks, and, particularly where a jury is involved, it is customarily a single continuous process without prolonged adjournment. Where the plaintiff seeks compensatory money damages, there is generally a right to jury trial, although this right may be waived. Jurors are not noted for their skill in coping with complex and involved transactions and, for this or for other reasons, both parties may prefer to put their case solely in the hands of a judge. Assuming, however, that trial is to be by jury, the jurors, twelve in number, are selected by lot from a larger group of qualified citizens, a cross section of the community, who have been summoned for jury duty.[10] Jurors sit for a single

---

[9] Judges in the United States wear black robes, but no wigs or caps. Lawyers and jurors wear business suits.

[10] The trial jury is the petit or petty jury, often called simply "the jury," as distinguished from the grand jury, discussed at p. 110 *infra*.

case only and are paid a modest amount to cover expenses. They must meet minimum requirements which relate to such matters as citizenship, eligibility as a voter, age, general health, and impartiality. Prospective jurors are subjected to what is known as a *voir dire* examination on their qualifications and may be challenged for cause by either party and excluded if they are not qualified. In addition each party has a number of peremptory challenges which he may use to exclude a juror without any stated reasons. After the jurors have been sworn to try the issues, they are seated in the jury box, and the trial begins. It is the task of the jury, at least in theory, to decide issues of "fact," and that of the judge to decide issues of "law." The dividing line between the two is often a shadowy one, and, for example, whether the jury's decision on an issue of "fact" has been reasonable is itself an issue of "law."

The plaintiff has the initial burden of presenting evidence in support of his claim. First, both parties make opening statements in which they explain their side of the case to the jury so that it will be better able to follow the proof. In some jurisdictions, however, the defendant's opening is not made until he is about to begin to prove his case. The plaintiff then proceeds to prove his case. This he traditionally does by oral rather than written evidence, although documentation may be voluminous in large cases where business records are involved. One consequence of the adversary system is that witnesses are called on behalf of the parties themselves and not on behalf of the court. The court may by subpoena order a party who is within the court's territorial jurisdiction to appear and give testimony or to produce a writing or object, if he will not do so voluntarily. The parties themselves are generally competent to testify. The first witness for the plaintiff is called to the witness stand for direct examination and is sworn to tell the truth. His testimony is elicited by questions posed by the plaintiff's lawyer. It is the practice of lawyers in the United States to discuss with their clients' witnesses their testimony in advance of trial in order to prevent waste of time and surprise at trial. It is, of course, improper for a lawyer to use this occasion to manipulate the testimony of the witness. After direct examination the defendant's lawyer is permitted to cross-examine the witness to show additional facts or inconsistencies or to attack the witness's credibility. Because the witness has been called on behalf of the plaintiff, the right to cross-examination is an important one. There may then be redirect and recross examination. The judge may also question the witness, but the burden of examination is on the opposing lawyers. Other witnesses are then called and documents and physical objects may be presented. These are subject to the rules of evidence, however, and, for example, the results of the pre-trial procedure, such as depositions and documents, are not necessarily admissible at the trial. After presenting his proof, the plaintiff will rest his case.

At this point the plaintiff must have introduced enough evidence on all issues as to which he has the burden of proof to justify a jury verdict for him.[11] The defendant may test whether he has done so by a motion that the action be dismissed. This is known in some jurisdictions as a motion that the plaintiff be nonsuited or that a verdict be directed for the defendant. The issue raised is only whether a reasonable jury could, on the basis of the plaintiff's evidence, reach a verdict in his favor. This is therefore regarded as an issue of "law" rather than one of "fact" and the judge alone passes upon the motion. If it is granted, the dismissal ends the trial and operates as a judgment on the merits for the defendant. If it is denied, the defendant must proceed with his case.

The defendant will then present his evidence in the same manner as did the plaintiff. This time the latter will have the right of cross-examination. At the conclusion of the defendant's case, the plaintiff may offer proof in rebuttal. At the close of all the evidence either party may move for a directed verdict on the ground that a reasonable jury could only return a verdict in his favor. This motion is also considered to raise a question of "law" rather than one of "fact." If the judge grants the motion the trial will end and judgment will be entered for the moving party. Under modern practice the judge no longer actually goes through the formality of directing the jury to bring in the appropriate verdict. If he denies the motion, the trial will proceed to its conclusion.

Both parties will then make their closing arguments to the jury. In some jurisdictions the plaintiff's closing is first, followed by the defendant's closing, then by the plaintiff's rebuttal. In

---

[11] The allocation of the burden of proof is therefore a matter of no small importance. The various meanings of the term "burden of proof" are untangled in Morgan, Maguire, and Weinstein, *Cases and Materials on Evidence* 417-23 (4th ed. 1957). For a brief discussion of the effect of presumptions, see *id.* 438-43.

others the defendant's closing is first, followed by the plaintiff's closing. Arguments must be confined to the evidence which has been presented and each side will attempt, by analysis of the proof, to persuade the jury that it should decide the case in its favor. The judge will then charge the jury by instructing it in the rules of law under which it is to reach its decision. Before closing argument, both sides may submit to the judge instructions which they propose that the judge give, and the judge will then disclose to them the instructions which he intends to give so that they can frame their argument accordingly. In some jurisdictions, however, the charge is given before the closing argument. The authority of the judge was reduced during the nineteenth century as a result of confidence in the average man's abilities as a juror and of unpleasant recollections of arbitrary and absolute judges who were supposed to have represented crown control during colonial times. The narrower role of the judge has resulted in a wider one for the jury, and indirectly for the opposing lawyers. One symptom of this is the rule in most states that the charge must not contain any comment on the weight of the evidence or the credibility of the witnesses, but must be confined to the rules of law to be applied. In many states the judge is not even permitted to summarize the evidence and in some he may not charge the jury orally but must do so in writing. These limitations have been much criticized by the organized bar, however, and the trend is now toward an expansion of the judge's role. Where the trial has been without a jury there is, of course, no charge, but the judge may, on motion, state the rules of law which he considers to be applicable.

After the charge, the jurors retire to the jury room where they deliberate in secret for a matter of hours and sometimes days, until they reach their verdict. In a civil case the jury must be persuaded "by a preponderance of the evidence," or in other words that the existence of the contested fact is more probable than not. Historically the verdict of the twelve jurors had to be unanimous, but this rule has generally been altered by constitution or statute. In some jurisdictions, however, less than a unanimous verdict is possible only with the consent of the parties. The "hung" jury, one unable to reach a decision by the required majority, is nevertheless highly unusual. The jury may be polled by asking each juror in open court whether he agrees with the verdict in order to make certain that the required number of jurors consent. No record is kept of their deliberations and rules severely restrict jurors from testifying to impeach their own verdict. The jury's verdict may be a general one, that is simply a finding for one side with an assessment of damages where appropriate; or the jury may be required to render a special verdict, in answer to specific questions of fact put to it by the judge, on the basis of which the judge will reach a decision. In some places the foreman of the jury gives the verdict orally. In others a written verdict signed by the foreman is returned and the jury gives oral assent when it is read in court. After receiving the verdict, the judge discharges the jury, and the trial is ended. If there has been no jury the judge makes findings of fact and conclusions of law. He may also write an opinion. Where there are equitable as well as legal questions of fact, the judge will answer the former himself rather than refer them to the jury.

After the jury verdict, the losing party may move for a new trial on a variety of grounds, including prejudicial error by the judge in ruling on the admissibility of evidence or in instructing the jury, or a verdict which is against the weight of the evidence. If the judge concludes that the damages awarded by the jury are unreasonably low or high, he may, by devices such as additur or remittitur, add or subtract an appropriate amount and order a new trial if the change is not accepted by the parties. The losing party may also make a motion for judgment notwithstanding the verdict (*non obstante veredicto*) in order to permit the judge to give him judgment on the merits where the judge had denied an earlier motion to direct a verdict in his favor. The grounds of the earlier and the later motions are the same. The judge may be more willing to grant a motion to give judgment as a matter of law after the jury has reached its verdict because, should his granting of the motion be reversed on appeal, there is then a verdict upon which the appellate court can enter judgment and it will save the time and expense of a new trial. The judge will also have had more time to deliberate before passing on a motion for judgment nothwithstanding the verdict. Finally, assuming that all motions made after the verdict was rendered have been denied, the judge will enter judgment on the verdict. The judgment will ordinarily require the losing party to pay the costs of the successful party. These include such fees as those paid to the court by the successful party, but do not include his lawyer's fee. If the losing party refuses to pay a money judgment, a number of procedures are available by way of execution; for example, his property may be seized by a court officer and sold at a public sale to pay the judgment.[12]

CHARACTERISTICS — APPEAL

After the trial, a party may appeal from the judgment, claiming error on the part of the trial judge. During the appeal, execution of judgment can be suspended upon the posting of a bond by the appellant. Ordinarily the appellant must be able to show that he tried to protect his rights at the appropriate time during the trial, by making or opposing a motion, by raising an objection, or by taking other steps to bring the matter to the attention of the judge. By the end of the trial the judge will have ruled on a variety of such contested points—motions attacking pleadings, objections to the admission or exclusion of evidence, motions for a directed verdict, and so on. The appeal will usually be based on one or more of these rulings. Whether the losing party may appeal from interlocutory rulings which are not finally dispositive of the case will vary from state. Some, for example, will not allow appeal from an order sustaining or overruling a motion to dismiss for failure to state a cause of action, with the result that the aggrieved party must refrain from pleading over and submit to a judgment in order to have an appellate review of the ruling. The party who appeals is called the appellant or petitioner or plaintiff-in-error; the other party is the appellee or respondent or defendant-in-error.

There is no new trial, no jury, no witnesses, in the appellate court. The judges' knowledge of the case is derived solely from the record, a stenographic transcript of the proceedings in the lower court, that shows the asserted errors of the trial judge. The appellate court is aided by detailed written briefs prepared by the parties in support of their cases. When the question on appeal is of importance beyond the immediate parties themselves, the court may also have before it a brief *amicus curiae* by a "friend of the court" such as the government or an interested private group. Oral proceeding are limited to questions of "law," and the parties will urge upon the court those precedents and other authorities that they regard as controlling. The court will

---

[12] This officer in the state courts is a sheriff, a county official, and in the federal courts is a United States Marshal.

not intrude upon the province of the jury as trier of issues of "fact," but it may determine that the jury exceeded the bounds of reasonableness in reaching its verdict if this issue has been raised by a proper motion before the trial judge. The appellate court will be reluctant to reach such a conclusion, however, where the judge and jury have had the opportunity of observing key witnesses when they testified. The decision of the court, usually accompanied by a written opinion, may not be handed down for weeks or even months while the judges study the briefs and confer among themselves. If the court finds that there was no error, or if there was error that it was "harmless" and probably did not affect the outcome, it will affirm the judgment below. If it finds reversible error, it will reverse the judgment and remand the case either for entry of judgment for the appellant or for a new trial, depending on the circumstances. If the case is remanded, the lower court is bound to follow the instructions of the appellate court. The costs of the appeal, which again fall short of actual expenses, are borne by the losing party and the expense of appeals tends to limit the number of litigants who seek review.

Suggested Readings

There is no general treatise on American civil procedure. Karlen, *Primer of Procedure* (1950) is a readable one-volume introduction, designed for entering law students, and contains a typical record of trial, including sample documents. Similar materials together with cases and comment are collected in a recent casebook, Rosenberg and Weinstein, *Elements of Civil Procedure* (1962). Blume, *American Civil Procedure* (1955) is a short introductory work. Clark, *Handbook of the Law of Code Pleading* (2nd ed. 1947) is a useful volume on pre-trial procedure. Of the many works devoted to the law of procedure in a single jurisdiction, the most important are *Moore's Federal Practice* (2nd ed.), in eight loose-leaf volumes with current supplements, and Barron and Holtzoff, *Federal Practice and Procedure (Civil and Criminal) with Forms* (Rules ed. by Wright 1958), in seven volumes with current pocket supplements, still in the process of revision. A one-volume loose-leaf work on federal civil procedure is Moore and Vestal, *Moore's Manual— Federal Practice and Procedure.* Two books on the history of civil procedure in the United States are Millar, *Civil Procedure of the Trial Court in Historical Perspective* (1952) and Pound, *Appellate Procedure in Civil Cases* (1941).

CRIMINAL PROCEDURE

SCOPE AND SOURCES

The law of criminal procedure has been affected, to a much greater extent than that of civil procedure, by both federal and state constitutions. In detail it is largely statutory in form and varies considerably from one jurisdiction to the next. Field's code of criminal procedure was less influential a unifying force than was his code of civil procedure; a Model Code of Criminal Procedure proposed by the American Law Institute in 1930 has had only limited success as an instrument of reform; and the Federal Rules of Criminal Procedure promulgated by the Supreme Court of the United States in 1946 have had less impact on the states than have the Rules of Civil Procedure. The procedure varies not only with the jurisdiction but also with the seriousness of the crime. In any case, the purpose of the proceedings is solely the punishment of crime. Redress of private injury occasioned by the criminal act is available only in separate civil proceedings. The discussion which follows concerns a typical prosecution for one of the more serious crimes known as felonies; petty offenses are tried by a more summary procedure.

CHARACTERISTICS

Criminal procedure in America is essentially accusatory, with the prosecutor taking the leading role, rather than inquisitorial, with the judge taking the leading role. The trial of criminal, even more than civil, cases reflects the adversary nature of the judicial process and confidence in the capacities of laymen as jurors. On the one side stands the prosecutor, an elected official or a political appointee, whose extraordinary powers and discretion are one of the chief characteristics of the administration of criminal justice in the United States. On the other stands the person accused of crime, who is protected against abuses on the part of the prosecutor and the police by equally extraordinary constitutional safeguards which may require the reversal of a conviction for the most technical departures from the requirements of due process. [13] Between them stand judges and jurors, as impartial arbiters.

The first official step in most criminal cases is the arrest by a police officer of the person suspected of the crime. The suspect must, without unnecessary delay, be brought before a judicial officer, known as a magistrate, who will conduct the preliminary examination. This is an informal public hearing to determine whether the evidence is sufficient to warrant holding the suspect. If the proceeding is not one of the very substantial proportion dismissed at this stage, the magistrate will fix bail as security for the suspect's release from custody. The hearing is not inquisitorial and the magistrate does not interrogate the suspect. The preparation of the prosecution's case is left entirely to the prosecutor. There is sometimes a tendency for the police to prolong the period between arrest and preliminary examination in order to question the suspect before he has seen a lawyer. Improper pressure by the police at this stage is popularly known as the "third degree". The suspect has, however, the constitutional privilege of refusing to answer questions and undue delay in bringing him before the magistrate may be a factor in determining whether there has been a violation of due process.

Formal accusation, designed to inform the accused of the charges against him, may be made in many states by either indictment or information. An indictment is an accusation framed by the prosecutor and found by a grand jury,[14] a panel of laymen who have heard only the evidence for the prosecution, to be

---

[13] As a matter of constitutional law, the Supreme Court of the United States has held that evidence obtained by an unreasonable search and seizure or a coerced confession is inadmissible in both the federal and state courts. A conviction obtained on such evidence or confession must be reversed even though there is abundant independent evidence of guilt. Other types of illegally obtained evidence are also inadmissible in the federal and some of the state courts. The controversial subject of wire tapping has been held to be outside of the protection of the federal Constitution, but is the subject of a federal statute and also of statutes in some states.

[14] In some states the grand jury may be composed of as many as twenty-three members, as opposed to the twelve member trial or petit jury. It is empowered to compel witnesses to attend and to testify under oath, and because of this power the prosecutor may prefer to proceed by indictment rather than by information. The suspect is not present and the proceedings are kept secret, in part to protect the reputation of the suspect should the grand jury decide not to indict, and in part to prevent premature disclosure of the prosecution's case to the suspect. The grand jury need not be unanimous. Traditionally it has also had broad authority to investigate on its own initiative and it may be empowered to make its own independent accusation in the form of a presentment.

sufficiently justified to be sent on to trial. In many jurisdictions indictment by a grand jury has given way to a simpler procedure in which a formal accusation, known as an information, is filed by the prosecutor.

The indictment or information is followed by arraignment before the trial judge, the formal reading of the charge to the accused in open court followed by his oral plea of "guilty" or "not guilty". Generally the accused need not indicate the nature of his defense. He may also object on a variety of grounds to the legal sufficiency of the accusation. Or he may plead guilty to a lesser offense than that charged. And in some jurisdictions he may plead *"nolo contendere"*, which authorizes judgment and sentence just as a plea of guilty would, but which may not be considered an admission of guilt and used against him in other criminal or civil proceedings. Pleas of guilty are entered in the great majority of cases. Many are obtained by concessions from the prosecutor to accept a plea of guilty to a lesser offense than charged or to recommend leniency in the sentence. If, however, the plea is not guilty, both sides prepare for trial. Pre-trial discovery procedure is much more limited than in civil cases, although the accused is sometimes given a list of witnesses to be called by the prosecution.

Trial is commonly before a judge sitting with a jury, although in most jurisdictions the defendant may agree to waive his constitutional right to jury trial. Not only are trials of criminal cases open to the public, but the case may be the subject of almost unrestricted comment by news media before and during trial. Although publicity may help to ensure a fair trial, the possible effect upon the jury of prejudicial reports poses a serious and unresolved problem which is of growing concern to the bench and bar. The procedure at trial does not differ greatly from that of a civil action.[15] The defendant is competent to take the witness stand and testify, as might any other witness,

---

[15] The defendant is ordinarily represented by a lawyer. A lawyer in private practice may take or refuse the case of an accused person, as he may any client, without regard to his belief in his innocence. The Constitution has been construed to require that a lawyer be furnished to an indigent defendant charged with a felony in either a state or a federal court. During the trial the defendant is permitted to sit with his lawyer and to speek freely with him. The prosecutor sits on the same level as the defense and wears a business suit, as does the defense lawyer.

in his own behalf, but he can not be compelled to do so[16] and failure to testify creates no presumption against him and generally may not be commented upon by the prosecution. The presentation of evidence in open court, first for the prosecution, then for the defense, is followed by arguments for both sides, the judge's charge to the jury, its deliberation and verdict of guilty or not guilty, and the judgment of the court. All evidence is presented in open court. There is no file or *dossier* prepared before trial for the private use of judge or jury. As in civil actions, witnesses are interrogated one at a time and do not confront each other, and it is the practice of each side to question its witnesses in advance of trial. The jury will be instructed that they must acquit unless they are convinced of guilt "beyond a reasonable doubt," and their verdict must be unanimous. After judgment, if the accused is convicted, sentence is imposed within limits set by statute, usually by the judge but sometimes by the jury. It may, depending upon the gravity of the offense, consist of a fine, imprisonment, or, at least in most states, death. The defendant may appeal from a conviction and the appellate court may, if it reverses, order a new trial, but because of constitutional protections of the defendant against double jeopardy, it is an almost universal rule that the prosecution may not seek reversal of an acquittal. Only a few American jurisdictions, however, have enacted statutes which give the convicted defendant who has served part of his sentence the right to damages upon a later finding of not guilty. But while the small minority of cases which go to trial attract the public's attention, the overwhelming majority of criminal proceedings are disposed of without trial, largely by dismissal on preliminary examination and by plea of guilty on arraignment.

Suggested Readings

The best introductory book is Puttkammer, *Administration of Criminal Law* (1953). Two more extensive studies are Orfield, *Criminal Procedure from Arrest to Appeal* (1947) and Orfield, *Criminal Appeals in America* (1939). Moreland, *Modern Criminal Procedure* (1959) is a one-volume treatise.

---

[16] The Fifth Amendment to the federal Constitution provides that, "No person . . . shall be compelled in any criminal case to be a witness against himself . . . ," and many state constitutions contain similar provisions. In spite of this language, the so-called "privilege against self-incrimination" extends to all judicial or official hearing, inquiries, or investigations where a person is called upon formally to give testimony.

EVIDENCE

SCOPE AND SOURCES

The law of evidence deals with such matters as the kinds of judicial proof, the competency and examination of witnesses, the admission and exclusion of evidence, privileges, burdens of proof, and presumptions. It is found largely in judicial decisions and varies from state to state for, with the exception of a few special statutes and an occasional relevant provision from codes or rules of procedure, it has not yet submitted to either legislation or unification.[17] In 1942 the American Law Institute attempted to remedy this situation by promulgating a Model Code of Evidence, but it was not adopted in any jurisdiction. In 1953 the National Conference of Commissioners on Uniform State Laws recomended the Uniform Rules of Evidence, which are being considered for adoption in a number of jurisdictions. With some exceptions the rules of evidence in criminal cases are fundamentally the same as those in civil cases.[18]

CHARACTERISTICS

Like the rest of the law of procedure, the law of evidence bears the stamp both of the adversary character of litigation and of the institution of the jury. In keeping with the contentious nature of the proceeding, the initiative is on the parties rather than the judge both to develop the evidence and police its admission. They bear the sole responsibility for producing the proof, and, decisions on issues of fact are based exclusively on evidence brought forth in open court. Some facts, however, may be such common knowledge that the court will take judicial notice of them, without proof. Traditionally, testimony is elicited question by question; documents are submitted item by item and not in mass, although this practice as to documents is changing, particularly in large cases where quantities of business records are involved. The tradition enables the other party to make prompt objection, often when the question is asked or when the item is proffered, if he would have the evidence excluded from

---

[17] The Federal Rules of Civil Procedure contain a liberal provision which makes evidence admissible in the federal courts if it is admissible under either federal law or the law of the state in which the court sits.

[18] Compare, however, the burden of persuasion "by a preponderance of evidence" in civil cases with that "beyond a reasonable doubt" in criminal cases. See pp. 105, 112 *supra*.

the consideration of the jury. Failure to do so is ordinarily a waiver of the objection. Particularly where there is a jury, the judge will usually rule upon objections without hearing argument in order to avoid delay and to preserve continuity. Although the aggrieved party may appeal an erroneous ruling, the trial judge is accorded considerable discretion and the appellate court will reverse only if it concludes that there is a substantial probability that an improper ruling influenced the verdict or finding below.

Another result of the adversary nature of the proceeding is that witnesses are called on behalf of the parties rather than on behalf of the court. Not only are the parties expected to produce their own lay witnesses, but their own expert witnesses as well, including, for example, medical doctors, scientists and engineers, handwriting and ballistics experts, and experts in foreign law.[19] The result is not infrequently a battle of experts in which each adversary is represented by a battery of specialists, compansated by him, and selected, at least in part, because their testimony will be favorable. Each specialist is required to submit to cross-examination by the opposing party. Dissatisfaction with this system has begun to produce change. One of the purposes of the pre-trial conference may be to limit the number of expert witnesses, and a few courts have gone further and appointed neutral experts in addition to those called by the parties.

A second factor, the institution of the jury, has also had a pervasive influence on the law in this field. Although the highly refined rules of evidence have developed largely in order to control the jury, the rules devised for the jury system have affected all trials. A judge sitting without a jury does have a discretionary power to depart from the rules for jury trial; and conversely a judge sitting with a jury must be particularly careful to exclude as "irrelevant" evidence which has no probative value on contested issues. But the courts have not developed a distinct set of rules for non-jury cases.

A particularly important result of the jury system is that, beyond the exclusion of irrelevant evidence, there are some rules which exclude relevant evidence on the ground that its value is outweighed by the danger that the jury may give it too much weight. This policy is at the root of that most notorious of all

---

[19] Lay witnesses are, within the bounds of reason, required to state "facts," that is to describe what they observed, rather than give "opinions." The jury is expected to draw its own inferences. This "opinion rule," which has been increasingly relaxed in recent years, does not apply to expert witnesses.

exclusionary rules of evidence, the hearsay rule. In general terms, this rule, which is subject to many exceptions, excludes evidence of any statement made out of court where the statement is offered for the purpose of proving a matter which the statement asserts. Accordingly, a witness will not be allowed to prove the occurrence of an event by testifying that someone else told him that the event took place.[20] The conventional justification of the rule is that the judge or juror, who it must be remembered comes to the trial with no prior knowledge of the facts, can form a reliable impression of the truthfulness of a witness by observing his demeanor as he testifies, particularly under cross-examination. Because the out-of-court statement was made out of the sight of judge and jurors at a time when there was no opportunity to cross-examine its author, hearsay evidence is thought to be of doubtful reliability. Instead of receiving it and leaving its evaluation to the jurors, is it excluded lest they give it too much credence.

The hearsay rule operates to exclude written as well as oral statements made out of court and thus has contributed to the tradition of oral testimony in open court.[21] Even the exception which permits the admission of depositions is in many instances conditioned upon the unavailability of the deponent as a witness. And the exception which allows the admission of business records was long restricted to situations where the person who made the record was not available to testify. This limitation has now been abolished in a majority of states by adoption of the Uniform Business Records as Evidence Act. Although the present tendency is clearly toward relaxation of the exclusionary rules, efforts have been directed at reformation of the rules rather than at a fundamental shift in the methods of proof. It is only fair to admit that litigation in the United States is, and will probably remain, appreciably more costly and time-consuming because of its adversary nature and its jury tradition.

SUGGESTED READINGS

The standard work on evidence is Wigmore, *A Treatise on*

---

20 For example, a witness will not be permitted to testify that A said that B committed a crime in order to prove that B committed the crime. But the rule does not prevent the witness from testifying that A said that B committed the crime in order to prove that A actually made such a statement and so is liable to B for defamation.

21 With few exceptions, any person, including a party, is generally competent to testify.

the Anglo-American System of Evidence (3rd ed. 1940) in ten volumes with pocket supplements, now in the process of revision. The best one-volume texts are McCormick, *Handbook on the Law of Evidence* (1954), and Morgan, *Basic Problems of Evidence* (1961). Maguire, *Evidence—Common Sense and Common Law* (1947) is a short introductory book on the principles behind the law of evidence. Morgan, *Some Problems of Proof Under the Anglo-American System of Litigation* (1956) is a useful monograph based on a series of lectures. A volume of *Selected Writings on the Law of Evidence and Trial* (1957) has been published under the sponsorship of the Association of American Law Schools.

CONFLICT OF LAWS

Scope and Sources

The subject matter of conflict of laws, as private international law is known in the United States, consists primarily of jurisdiction, enforcement of foreign judgments, and choice of law. Because there was no developed law in this field in England at the time of the Revolution, American judges and writers drew at first upon works of civil law authors.[22] Subsequent development was largely at the hands of the courts and each state now has its own conflict of laws rules, found for the most part in cases and to a lesser extent in statutes, including some uniform laws. As was mentioned earlier, these rules are binding on the federal courts in diversity cases. There are also several notable clauses of the federal Constitution which affect conflict of laws, as well as occasional federal statutes and, in the international sphere, treaties.

Characteristics

The subject is of great importance in interstate as well as in international situations, and, in general, the states have applied the same rules to both. Although the American people are highly mobile and business and social affairs are conducted in disregard of state boundaries, each state has its own local law and, to a marked degree, its own sovereignty. Because of this,

---

[22] See fn. 14, p. 11 *supra* for mention of Justice Story's treatise on conflict of laws, the first on this subject in the English language.

conflicts arise with far greater frequency and the subject is characterized by more refinement and detail than in other countries. The authors of the Constitution, sensitive to the possibility of chaos, included a number of provisions relating to conflict of laws, and the constitutional cast of the subject is perhaps its most striking feature.

Under the Constitution, the federal government itself is given limited powers in this sphere, including the treaty power and the power to legislate in specified areas. But the most important constitutional provisions are those which restrict the states. Of these, two are of special significance: first, the due process clause of the Fourteenth Amendment, which provides that no state shall "deprive any person of life, liberty, or property, without due process of law";[23] and second, the full faith and credit clause, which requires that each state must give "Full Faith and Credit" to the "public Acts, Records, and judicial Proceedings of every other State." As to these restrictions, which affect chiefly the law of jurisdiction and the enforcement of foreign judgments, the Supreme Court of the United States has the final voice.

The earliest basis for personal jurisdiction recognized by American courts was, aside from consent, physical presence. A defendant can generally[24] be sued in any state where he can be found and served with process, even if he is there only temporarily and the cause of action has no connection with that state.[25] In addition many other bases for personal jurisdiction have now been developed by statute, including domicile in the state, doing business in the state, doing an act within the state, and even doing an act outside the state which causes consequences within the state. State jurisdictional rules are subject, however, to the due process clause. If the procedure for notice and for an opportunity to be heard does not meet the tests of reasonableness and "fair play and substantial justice" which the Supreme Court has laid down under that clause, a judgment based on that procedure will be void.

---

[23] The Fifth Amendment, which applies to the federal government, contains substantially the same language.

[24] This is not always true, as, for example, in the case of claims arising under the penal laws of another state. In such a case the state where the offense was committed must institute extradition proceedings to have the suspect returned.

[25] A court may decline to exercise jurisdiction under the doctrine of *forum non conveniens* if it is a seriously inappropriate forum and an appropriate forum is available.

Once a judgment has been rendered, the Constitution also affects its enforceability in other states. Under the full faith and credit clause the courts of one state are bound to give to a valid judgment of the courts of another state the same effect that it would have in the state of rendition.[26] The clause also applies as between state and federal courts. If, however, the court which rendered the judgment had no jurisdiction, so that the judgment would not be valid even in the state of rendition, the clause does not require its enforcement in any other state. The requirement of full faith and credit extends only to judgments of American courts and not to judgments rendered in foreign countries, which are enforceable only under the doctrine of comity, without compulsion. American courts have, however, been very liberal in enforcing these latter judgments as well.

Rules relating to choice of law are less affected by the Constitution. A state may violate the due process clause if it applies its own law to a state of facts which is not sufficiently connected with that state to make it reasonable to apply its law, but the full faith and credit clause has had little impact upon choice of law rules. For the most part these are found in case law and show close kinship to those of civil law countries.

SUGGESTED READINGS

The *Restatement of the Law of Conflict of Laws* (1934) is being replaced by the *Restatement of the Law of Conflict of Laws, Second,* now in tentative drafts. One volume texts are Ehrenzweig, *A Treatise on the Conflict of Laws* (1962); Goodrich, *Handbook of the Conflict of Laws* (3rd ed. 1949); Stumberg, *Principles of Conflict of Laws* (2nd ed. 1951); and Leflar, *The Law of Conflict of Laws* (1959). A volume of *Selected Readings on Conflict of Laws* (1956) has been published under the auspices of the Association of American Law Schools.

---

[26] A judgment based on a penal law is not, however, entitled to full faith and credit.

Chapter XI

Private Law

Private law in the United States, in spite of its fragmentation, can be grouped under six major headings: contracts, torts, property, family law, commercial law, and business enterprises. What do these fields encompass and what are their principal characteristics?

CONTRACTS

Scope and Sources

The law of contracts is concerned with the enforcement of promissory obligations. Contractual liability is usually based on consent freely given in the form of an express promise or one implied in fact from the acts of the parties. In some circumstances, however, the courts will imply a promise (often called implied in law or quasi contract) in order to avoid unjust enrichment in spite of lack of consent by the party who is bound by it.[1]

The subject matter of contract law comprises capacity, formalities, offer and acceptance, consideration, fraud and mistake, legality, interpretation and construction, performance and conditions of performance, frustration and impossibility, discharge, rights of assignees and third party beenficiaries, and remedies. It has, to a very considerable extent, preserved its unitary quality, resisting fundamental distinctions between different classes of contracts according to either the subject of the agreement or the nature of the parties. Accordingly, with some exceptions, its principles are applicable to agreements on such varied subjects as employment, sale of goods or land, and insurance, and to such diverse

---

[1] For example, a doctor who renders emergency treatment to an unconscious person is entitled to recoyer on such a promise.

parties as individuals, business organizations, and governmental entities.

It is largely state rather than federal law, but it differs usually only in detail from one state to another. While it is still primarily case law, an increasing number of statutes deal with particular problems. The Uniform Commercial Code, for example, contains some special provisions on the formation of contracts for the sale of goods. And by the Tucker Act of 1887, as amended, one of the most significant of the federal statutes in the field, the United States government has waived its sovereign immunity in contract actions by consenting to suit in the federal courts. Some rules laid down by statute, and by case law as well, are mandatory or compulsory and cannot be avoided by the parties, while others are implicative, interpretative, or suppletory and can be varied by agreement.

CHARACTERISTICS

A contract may be simply defined as a promise for the breach of which the law gives a remedy,[2] although the word "contract" may also be used to refer to the series of acts by which the parties expressed their agreement, to the document which they may have executed, or to the legal relations which have resulted. Not all promises are enforceable and several criteria must be met before the law will give a remedy. Two of the most fundamental of these are the requirement of a writing and the requirement of consideration. The requirement of a writing is imposed by statutes of frauds, derived from the English Statute of Frauds of 1677, which have been enacted throughout the United States. Typically they provide that, with some exceptions, specified kinds of contracts are unenforceable unless evidenced by a writing.[3] They usually cover contracts to sell goods of more than a minimum value, contracts to sell land, contracts to answer for the debt of another, and contracts not to be performed within a year. Many agreements, such as most contracts to furnish services, are not included and are enforceable even if there is no writing. Although dissatisfaction has led to the repeal

---

[2] This is essentially the definition of the *Restatement on Contracts* §1.

[3] They do not, however, require that the contract itself be written and do not, therefore, exclude evidence of oral statements once a writing has been produced which satisfies the minimum requirements of the statute. The parol evidence rule, however, may operate to severely limit evidence of prior or contemporary oral, or even written, statements where the contract is embodied in a writing which purports to be complete.

of most of the English Statute of Frauds in 1954, there has been no serious movement for its abolition in the United States.

Apart from any requirement of a writing, a promise is not generally enforceable in the United States unless it is supported by consideration. Historically a promisor could make a binding written promise, even without consideration, by affixing his wax seal to the writing. But as the wax seal was replaced by a penned or printed imitation, the seal became an empty formality and its effectiveness has now been eliminated or at least greatly diminished by state statutes. Consideration is essentially something for which the promisor has bargained and which he has received in exchange for his own promise. It may be another promise given in return, in which case the resulting contract is known as a bilateral contract, or it may be an act given in return, in which case the resulting contract is known as a unilateral contract. But, for example, a gratuitous promise, including one to pay for goods or services which have already been furnished at the time the promise is made, is not supported by consideration. Fortunately there are only a few such instances of business promises in which the requirement of consideration is not met. One of the most troublesome involves the "firm," or irrevocable, offer. The usual rule in the United States is that an offeror has the power to revoke his offer at any time before its acceptance by the offeree, and a promise by the offeror not to revoke is not generally effective unless supported by consideration. A common device for holding the offeror to his promise is the payment to him of a nominal sum, for example one dollar,[4] as consideration for what is then known as an "option." Even without consideration a few courts have held that the offeror was estopped, or precluded, from revoking his offer where the offeree relied to his detriment upon the promise. But the most satisfactory solution has been through legislation, adopted in a number of states, making an offer irrevocable, regardless of consideration, if it is embodied in a signed writing which states that it is irrevocable. As this suggests, the tendency has been to attempt to remedy the deficiencies of the doctrine of consideration rather than to discard it.

In the United States, contracts, like statutes, are characteristically detailed and prolix. Those prepared by lawyers are often compounded of standard clauses, popularly known as "boiler-

---

[4] Traditionally, the doctrine of consideration has not insisted upon adequacy or fairness in the exchange.

plate," taken from other agreements kept on file or from form books. Even when a lawyer is not directly involved, the parties may use or incorporate by reference a standard printed form which has been drafted by a lawyer, perhaps for a particular enterprise, perhaps for an association of enterprises, or perhaps for sale to the general public. This attention to detail may be due to a number of causes, including the standardization of routine transactions, the frequent involvement of lawyers in all stages of exceptional transactions, the inclination to use language which has been tested in previous controversies, and the desire to avoid uncertainty when the law of more than one state may be involved. All of these add to the general disposition of the case-oriented American lawyer to provide expressly for specific disputes which have arisen in the past or which might be foreseen in the future.

A related phenomenon is the widespread use of standard form "contracts of adhesion," such as tickets, leases, and retail sales contracts, which are forced upon the party with inferior bargaining power. In recent years, courts and legislatures have become increasingly concerned with the effects which unrestrained freedom of contract may have in such situations. Courts which had always refused to enforce agreements contemplating crimes, torts, or other acts which were clearly contrary to the public interest, began, under the guise of interpreting the contracts, to favor the weaker party and in extreme cases to deny effect to terms dictated by one party even where the subject of the agreement was not in itself unlawful. Legislatures enacted statutes fixing terms, such as maximum hours and minimum wages for employment, or even prescribing entire contracts, such as insurance policies, and gave administrative bodies the power to determine rates and conditions for such essential services as transportation and electricity. Nevertheless, in spite of the erosion of the doctrine of freedom of contract in many areas, the doctrine is still the rule rather than the exception.

Suggested Readings

The *Restatement of Contracts* (1933), now in the process of revision, and the *Restatement of Restitution* (1937) are both authoritative in this field. The classic treatises are *Corbin on Contracts* (1950-62), in eight volumes with periodic revisions and current pocket supplements, and Williston, *A Treatise on the*

Law of Contracts (3rd edition by Jaeger 1957-), a multi-volume work with current pocket supplements. Each of these is published in a one-volume abridgement. Another one-volume text is Simpson, *Handbook of the Law of Contracts* (1954). Simpson, *Handbook on the Law of Suretyship* (1950) deals with a special kind of contract. Other sources in related fields, including insurance, are listed below under Commercial Law.

TORTS

SCOPE AND SOURCES

The field of torts embraces a group of civil wrongs, other than breach of contract, which interfere with person, property, reputation, or commercial or social advantage. While an act, such as an assault, may sometimes be both a crime punishable by the state in a criminal prosecution and also a tort actionable by the victim in a suit for damages, the criminal prosecution and the damage action are entirely separate and unrelated proceedings. The essential purpose of the law of torts is compensatory and, although punitive damages may occasionally be awarded, its function is distinct from that of criminal law. Conversely, criminal law is essentially punitive and an injured party may not have compensation in the criminal proceeding.

Tort law is chiefly state rather than federal law and so varies somewhat throughout the country. Although it is predominantly case law rather than statute law,[5] most states have a variety of isolated statutes dealing with special problems. Common examples are the wrongful death acts and survival statutes which govern rights upon the death of the injured party.[6] One of the more significant federal statutes is the Federal Tort Claims Act of 1946 by which the United States has, with some exceptions, waived its sovereign immunity from liability for the torts of its employees so that recovery may now be had in a suit against the United States in the federal courts but without a jury, under circumstances where it would be liable if it were a private person.

---

[5] There are, of course, many statutes which prescribe a course of conduct and violation of such a statute may be used to show negligence as a matter of law.

[6] Wrongful death acts were enacted to reverse the prior case law rule that no action could be founded upon the death of a human being. Survival statutes were enacted to change the prior case law rule that personal tort actions did not survive the death of either the plaintiff or the defendant.

CHARACTERISTICS

Most torts can be divided into two broad categories depending on whether the result is intended or produced by negligence. In addition there are some injuries, such as those resulting from defamation[7] and from highly dangerous activities, for which there is absolute, or strict, liability without either intent or negligence. The intentional torts which cause interference with person or property include the classical torts that were adopted from English law with relatively few changes: assault, battery, conversion, false imprisonment, and trespass. An unreasonable interference, whether intentional or negligent, with another's use or enjoyment of land may also amount to a private nuisance, and such cases involving, for example, the creation of fumes or noise by one landowner to the detriment of his neighbors, have often been considered appropriate for equitable relief by way of injunction.[8] Intentional torts where the invasion is of a less tangible interest have undergone considerable judicial development in recent years; they include infliction of mental anguish, injurious falsehood, interference with contractual relations, malicious prosecution, misrepresentation, and invasion of the right of privacy, a tort of modern origin.[9] However, the vast bulk of tort litigation concerns claims for injuries negligently inflicted, often arising out of automobile accidents, and almost invariably involving personal injuries. They are economically the most significant tort cases and the damages awarded to a single plaintiff for personal injuries may be in the hundreds of thousands of dollars.[10]

The jury, which is almost universally employed in tort damage actions, has had its greatest impact in personal injury litigation. Because of the difficulty of isolating questions of law and keeping them from the jury, and because of the emotional involvement which jurors feel in such cases, jury practices are

---

[7] Defamation is generally libel if written, slander if spoken.

[8] Abatement of the nuisance by self-help, without court action, may also be permissible.

[9] On the origin of this tort, see p. 80 *supra*.

[10] Personal injury cases account for more than half of the private civil cases filed in the major trial courts. Compensatory damages in such cases may include allowance for medical expenses, pain and suffering, and loss of income and earning power, but not attorneys' fees. However, these cases are often handled by the lawyer for the plaintiff on a contingent fee basis under which his fee is fixed as a percentage of the recovery.

often at wide variance with the legal rules announced by the courts. In a negligence case, the jury will be instructed to decide whether the defendant's conduct met the standard of care expected of a reasonable man under similar circumstances. Unless it finds that the defendant failed to conform to this standard, it is not to allow recovery. But since the jury's verdict is, within wide limits, conclusive on this issue, there is little to prevent it from imposing nearly absolute liability, regardless of fault, upon a defendant who, because of ability to pay or to insure, can in the jurors' eyes best bear the loss. Similarly, although the United States is the last major stronghold of the common law doctrine of contributory negligence,[11] the doctrine has been seriously eroded by the jury system. Under this doctrine, even where the defendant has been negligent, he may avoid all liability by proving that the plaintiff's own negligence contributed to his loss. Since the relative degrees of fault of the two parties are immaterial, in theory there are only two alternatives: complete recovery if only the defendant has been negligent, and no recovery if neither or both of the parties have been negligent. In practice, however, these extreme results are tempered by the jury's power not only to determine whether the parties have been negligent but also to decide what damages, if any, are to be awarded. Accordingly, where a general verdict is returned, there is nothing to prevent the jury from ignoring the doctrine of contributory negligence by allowing recovery and then taking account of the plaintiff's negligence in calculating damages. Some judicial control can be exercised by use of the special verdict.[12]

The adequacy of traditional tort doctrines to cope with personal injury claims in an industrialized society has been the subject of considerable controversy. The widespread availability and use of private liability insurance has prompted suggestions of absolute liability for enterprises which typically cause injury. A number of states by statute require or encourage motor vehicle owners to so insure. But although jurors' attitudes are undoubtedly influenced by the likelihood of insurance, they are not told whether the defendant is insured in a particular case. Such considerations have made little impact on the general legal rules

---

[11] The doctrine has been entirely rejected in six states. It was abandoned in England in 1945 and has been rejected in special federal statutes governing railway and maritime workers.

[12] The special verdict is discussed briefly at p. 106 *supra*.

of liability for negligence. The most significant departure from orthodox tort law came with the enactment in every state of workmen's compensation statutes to cover personal injuries sustained by employees covered by statute in the course of their employment. The advantages to the employee are that where the accident is within the scope of the statute, the liability of the employer is absolute without regard to his negligence and such defenses as the employee's own contributory negligence are abolished. In return, workmen's compensation is made the employee's exclusive remedy against his employer. The employee loses the opportunity to sue the employer for negligence, and to seek a large verdict from a sympathetic jury, and must take instead a much smaller amount of compensation which is determined under a statutory formula. The employer is aided by a system of compulsory and usually private liability insurance for which he alone pays, and he is expected to transfer any additional cost to the consumer. The system is administered by a state administrative agency. In spite of its success and some obvious advantages, there is little likelihood that it will replace the conventional jury trial in the ordinary personal injury case.

Suggested Readings

Although the law of torts is not uniform, the *Restatement of Torts* (1934) contains an orderly compilation of the then prevailing views, and tentative drafts of the *Restatement of Torts, Second* have been published. The standard one-volume text, Prosser, *Handbook of the Law of Torts* (2nd ed. 1955), is by the reporter on torts of the *Restatement Second*. The most scholarly and original work is the three-volume treatise by Harper and James, *The Law of Torts* (1956).

PROPERTY

Scope and Sources

The roots of American property law are in the feudal land law of England. Accordingly, it distinguishes between real property, which historically consisted chiefly of feudally important estates in land, and personal property,[13] which consisted of most

---

[13] Personal property now includes, therefore, such intangibles as contract rights, including bank deposits and corporate stock, and industrial property, including patents and copyrights.

other assets, corporeal and incorporeal. Although the distinction persisted even after England had evolved into a commercial nation and personal property had taken on much greater importance, there has been a tendency in the United States toward its gradual elimination so that, for example, the rules of intestate succession are now largely the same for real and personal property. But since commercial dealings in personal property are embraced by the distinct field of commercial law, property law is still concerned primarily with real property. It includes: the kinds of interests in and types of ownership of property; conveyances, mortgages, and other *inter vivos* transfers of such interests; wills and intestate succession; trusts; and restrictions on the use of property.

Property law in the United States is a matter of peculiarly local concern and its variations from state to state are more substantial than is the case, for example, for contracts or torts. In several areas once under the rule of Spain or France, the influence of the civil law can still be detected, and eight states now recognize what is known as community property, in which husband and wife have a variety of common ownership that is derived from the civil law. Each state has a substantial collection of statutes relating to property, most notably on matters of intestate succession. Some are uniform acts adopted in a number of states, and others have been borrowed from sister states, particularly New York. Rarely, however, do these statutes form a well organized and integrated whole. Occasionally federal legislation, such as the United States Housing Acts, providing financial assistance for urban redevelopment, also affects the work of the property lawyer.

CHARACTERISTICS

The elaborate scheme of interests in land that distinguished English land law at the time of the Revolution was received almost in its entirety in the United States.[14] First, interests such as easements and franchises, which consist only of limitations on the rights of another to the possession and enjoyment of land, are distinguished from those interests which confer or may confer upon the holder the actual right to possession. The latter are then divided into possessory estates or interests, under which

---

[14] The English concept of tenure, under which all land was held ultimately from the king, had almost no influence in practice in the United States.

the holder has the present right to possession, and future or non-possessory estates or interests, under which the holder may or will come into possession at some future time. Possessory interests in turn are classified according to duration,[15] and future interests according to the probability or certainty of the holder coming into possession.[16] The common law has shown itself capable of remarkable abstraction in dealing with interests in land. Ownership is viewed as projected in time and may be divided according to the needs of the owner and the ingenuity of his lawyer, with the result that all persons who have estates, whether possessory or future, are present owners of vested interests in the land.[17]

The most significant departure from English property law after the Revolution related to title assurance. The standard instrument of land transfer in America is the deed, a writing historically under seal which passes title by delivery. It customarily contains a provision by which the transferror agrees to compensate the transferee for loss resulting from defective title. In England the transferee got further assurance by examination of the original deeds which were passed on with the land. A different system, that of public recordation, came into use in the colonies and subsequently spread throughout the United States. State recording acts require that all conveyances be promptly recorded in a local public office so that the prospective transferee may rely, with some safety, upon an examination, usually by a local expert, of the resulting public records. The penalty for failure to record is loss of priority to other competing interests, a matter on which the details of state statutes differ considerably. To an increasing extent the assurance from recordation is now being supplemented by a system of voluntary private title insurance in which the title insurer, after a search of the records, agrees to indemnify the insured for loss due to defective title.

---

[15] Examples are a fee simple absolute, which has a potentially infinite duration, a life estate, which has a duration fixed by the life or lives of one or more persons, and an estate for years, which is fixed in terms of years, months, weeks, or days.

[16] For example, the unconditional future interest left in the holder of an estate in fee simple absolute, after he has granted a life estate to another, is described as a reversion.

[17] Therefore, for example, the holder of the reversion mentioned in the preceding footnote is free to dispose of his interest as he might dispose of any property, either during his life or at his death, and thereby transfer the right to possession at some future time, even though he himself may die before the end of the outstanding life estate.

An alternative to recordation, known as title registration or the Torrens system,[18] exists to some degree in a minority of states. Under this system the title itself, rather than the conveyance evidencing the transfer of title, is registered through a formal proceeding that results in a conclusive determination of title followed by issuance by the state of a certificate of title, which is then kept up-to-date by notation of later interests. Expansion of title registration seems unlikely, however, in the face of the growth of title insurance based on recordation.

In recent decades the attention of the American property lawyer has turned increasingly from land transfer, and particularly the drafting of conveyances and wills, to restrictions on the use and enjoyment of land. The pressures of urban living have steadily increased as the percentage of city dwellers has grown from forty to sixty percent in the first half of this century and these pressures have been met by expanded governmental regulation, particularly on the local level. Under its power, known as the police power, to provide for the public welfare, the government may establish planning agencies, control the subdivision of land, restrict its use through zoning, and maintain minimum structural and sanitary standards. Under its power of condemnation, or eminent domain, it may also take private property for public uses, subject to the requirements of federal and state constitutions which include the payment of just compensation.[19] Judicial restraints on governmental power with respect to land use have been gradually relaxed, but questions still arise whether governmental action is a "taking" for which it must pay compensation, and if it is not, whether it is a valid exercise of the police power. In a nation where roughly sixty percent of all families own their own housing, such issues are of immediate and vital importance to a considerable portion of the population.

Suggested Readings

Much of the law of property is restated in the *Restatement of Property* (1936-44), the *Restatement of Trusts, Second* (1959),

---

[18] The system was named after Sir Robert Torrens, an Australian who introduced title registration there in the middle of the nineteenth century. It has since spread to most of the common law world outside the United States, including England.

[19] The Fifth Amendment to the federal Constitution prohibits the federal government from taking private property for public use without just compensation. The same limitation has been applied to the states under the due process clause of the Fourteenth Amendment.

and the *Restatement of Security* (1941). The leading work on real property, Powell, *The Law of Real Property,* in six loose-leaf volumes with current supplements, is by the reporter for the *Restatement of Property.* Casner (editor), *American Law of Property* (1952-54) is by numerous authors in seven volumes with current pocket supplements. Simes and Smith, *The Law of Future Interests* (2nd ed. 1956) is in four volumes with current pocket supplements and Simes, *Handbook on the Law of Future Interests* (1951) is in one volume. One-volume works on real property are Cribbet, *Principles of the Law of Property* (1962) and Burby, *Handbook of the Law of Real Property* (2nd ed. 1954). A single volume on personal property is Brown, *The Law of Personal Property* (2nd ed. 1955). Osborne, *Handbook on the Law of Mortgages* (1951) deals with mortgages, and Atkinson, *Handbook of the Law of Wills* (2nd ed. 1953) deals with wills and intestate succession. A longer work on wills is Bowe and Parker, *Page on Wills* (1960-   ), in eight volumes with current pocket supplements. The leading works on trusts are Scott, *The Law of Trusts* (2nd ed. 1956), in five volumes with current pocket supplements, by the reporter for both editions of the *Restatement of Trusts,* and Bogert, *The Law of Trusts and Trustees* (2nd ed. 1960-   ), in six volumes with current pocket supplements. One-volume works are Bogert, *Handbook of the Law of Trusts* (4th ed. 1963) and Scott, *Abridgment of the Law of Trusts* (1960).

FAMILY LAW

Scope and Sources

Family law, or domestic relations law as it is sometimes called, is concerned with the relationships between husband and wife and between parent and child, with the rights and duties which spring from these relationships, and with the status of married women and children. It is wholly state law since the federal government has no competence to make law in this field. Strongly influenced by English law during colonial times, it has everywhere been considerably altered by legislation and varies substantially from one state to another, although some uniformity has been achieved in limited areas through the adoption of uniform laws. In a number of jurisdictions it is administered by a separate family or domestic relations court, staffed with personnel who are specially trained in family problems.

CHARACTERISTICS

Marriage in the United States is fundamentally a relationship created by mutual consent of the spouses. All states provide by statute for the issuance of marriage licenses and some require a formal ceremony at which consent is solemnized before a clergyman or public official. Although many still recognize the alternative of a common law marriage, an informal marriage by mutual consent without license or ceremony, the actual number of common law marriages is relatively very small.[20] Common restrictions on capacity to marry relate to the age of the parties, the degree of their relationship, and, to an increasing extent, their physical condition, particularly as it may affect their offspring. A restriction can sometimes be circumvented by going to another state which has no such restriction, for a marriage which is valid in the state of celebration will ordinarily be recognized as valid by other states.

The marital relationship may be ruptured in three ways: by annulment, a court determination that no valid marriage existed between the parties; by separation, a judicial command that the parties live apart without severing the marriage bond;[21] and by divorce, a court decree dissolving the marital relationship, generally leaving the parties free to remarry. Divorce is the most common of these. In colonial times a marriage could be dissolved only by legislative act. After the Revolution, statutes were enacted in all states substituting judicial divorce on widely varying grounds, all of which required a showing of some serious fault on the part of the other spouse. The most usual grounds alleged are desertion and cruelty, which together account for a majority of all divorces. In keeping with the emphasis on fault, traditional defenses to divorce actions are: condonation, forgiveness of the fault by the complaining spouse; recrimination, fault on the part of the complaining spouse which would itself be grounds for divorce; collusion, fraudulent cooperation on the part of the complaining spouse, as by fabrication of evidence

---

20 Proxy or absentee marriages are not customary in the United States.

21 Judicial separation is the modern American form of the old decree of separation *a mensa et thoro*—from bed and board—as distinguished from the divorce *a vinculo matrimonii*—from the bonds of matrimony. It is not available in many states.

of fault; and connivance, consent by the complaining spouse to the other's fault. The tendency in modern legislation has been to liberalize the grounds of divorce to dispense with a showing of fault and permit divorce after voluntary separation for a number of years or occasionally upon a showing of incompatability.

Since the laws are designed for an adversary system in which divorce is granted in a contentious court proceeding, they may be easily circumvented by collusion between the spouses where, as in the great majority of cases, the action is not contested. In practice, consensual divorce is made possible by collusive practices throught the United States, and for this reason the alleged grounds are rarely the real cause of disintegration of the marriage. Only a minor fraction of all divorces is granted for adultery, although marital infidelity is the real cause in a much larger number of cases.

In a comparatively small number of instances in a few states where the grounds for divorce are severely limited,[22] the parties may choose the alternative of a so-called "migratory" divorce obtained in another state. The Supreme Court of the United States has held that domicile of one spouse alone is an adequate jurisdictional basis to entitle the divorce decree to full faith and credit. If the defendant has appeared in the divorce action, the court's own finding as to domicile can not later be attacked and every state must recognize the divorce. Since a wife may establish a domicile separate from that of her husband, a migratory divorce may be obtained by either spouse. A few states have commercialized migratory divorces by liberalizing grounds and relaxing residence requirements. The most popular is Nevada, where the court, after six weeks of residence by one of the spouses and an unchallenged affirmation that it is his or her intention to remain, will determine that the spouse is domiciled in Nevada so that it may grant a divorce. In spite of some recent attempts to get at the heart of the divorce problem by providing facilities for counselling and conciliation and by minimizing the adversary character of the proceedings, the divorce rate in the United States remains the highest in the world, and divorce continues to be one of the most unsatisfactory areas of American law.

The law has had more success in dealing with the rights of the spouses than with the preservation of their relationship.

---

[22] In New York, for example, adultery is the only ground for divorce.

Traditionally, under English law, the married woman was subject to a variety of legal disabilities which grew out of the view that husband and wife were one person and that authority was in the husband. For example, all of the wife's personal property as well as control of her real property went to the husband on marriage. Beginning in the nineteenth century, enactment of married women's property acts throughout the United States resulted in the emancipation of the wife by conferring upon her the right to her separate property, lifting her procedural disabilities, making explicit her power to contract, and, in some states, giving her the right of action for injury even as against her husband. The process has gone far, if unevenly, in most states, but little change has taken place in the corresponding burdens of the husband, notably that of support, even though he no longer takes control of his wife's property upon marriage. The wife may obtain a separate maintenance decree during the life of the marriage and the husband's obligation of support has been secured against avoidance by flight through universal enactment of the Uniform Reciprocal Enforcement of Support Act. Upon divorce, the support obligation may be replaced by an agreed upon lump settlement or by a court decree ordering the husband to make periodic payments of alimony. Alimony, which may be awarded both during and after the divorce lititation, is justified on alternative theories: either that it is in substitution for the suport obligation, or that it is in settlement for the dissolution of the marital partnership. At least traditionally, a court will not award alimony unless the wife is the "innocent" party. It is some indication of the inadequacy of legal procedures in meeting the fundamental problems of the marital relationship that in contested divorce cases it is usually the issue of support and not that of maintaining the relationship itself that is at the heart of the dispute.

SUGGESTED READINGS

There is a dearth of textwriting in this area. Madden, *Handbook of the Law of Persons and Domestic Relations* (1931) is a relatively old one-volume text. Vernier, *American Family Laws* (1931-38) is a five-volume treatise with 1938 supplement. Nelson, *Divorce and Annulment* (2nd ed. 1945, 1961) is in three volumes with current pocket supplements. A volume of *Selected*

Essays on Family Law (1950) has been published under the auspices of the Association of American Law Schools.

COMMERCIAL LAW

SCOPE AND SOURCES

The concept of "commercial law," or "commercial transactions" as it is sometimes called, as a distinct field is relatively recent in the United States. The practicing lawyer may still think of his practice as "commercial" to the extent that it involves any aspects of business, including even taxation, but the advent of the new Uniform Commercial Code has given a narrower ambit to the term "commercial." The preamble of the Code recites that it is concerned with "Certain Commercial Transactions in or regarding Personal Property and Contracts and other Documents concerning them." The subjects included are sale of goods, bulk sales, negotiable instruments (including promissory notes, bills of exchange or drafts, and checks), bank deposits and collections, letters of credit, documents of title (including stocks and bonds), and secured transactions (including pledges, chattel mortgages, conditional sales, trust receipts, and assignments of accounts receivable).

Commercial law in this sense is largely a matter of state law because, although Congress has the power to enact legislation concerning interstate commerce, it has been reluctant to exercise it in this sphere of private law. Its reluctance is due in part to the success of the National Conference of Commissioners on Uniform States Laws in promoting uniformity through voluntary adoption of uniform laws. The Negotiable Instruments Law, patterned after the English Bills of Exchange Act, was proposed in 1896 and adopted by all the states by 1924. The Uniform Sales Act, based in part on the English Sale of Goods Act, was recommended in 1906 and eventually adopted by about two thirds of the states. A succession of uniform laws followed.[23] At the end of the Second World War the Commissioners together with the American Law Institute undertook a joint project to draft a comprehensive and modern Uniform Commercial Code to replace the older uniform laws. It was proposed in final form in 1957, and has already been adopted in a substan-

---

[23] One of these, the Uniform Bills of Lading Act, was enacted by Congress as the Federal Bills of Lading, or Pomerene, Act to govern bills of lading in interstate and foreign commerce.

tial minority of states. It has four hundred sections,[24] fills over seven hundred pages with its elaborate comments, took dozens of draftsmen and advisors over a decade to prepare, and represents the most modern thinking in its field.

Although the Code unites in one statute such previously separate fields as sales and negotiable instruments,[25] it omits a number of subjects that are sometimes regarded as part of commercial law in other countries. Several of these, insurance is an example, have been omitted because of the difficulty of unification on so grand a scale. Others, such as bankruptcy and admiralty, or maritime law, have been left out because they are within federal rather than state jurisdiction.[26]   Still others, such as corporations and partnerships, are not included because the American lawyer sees no close affinity between them and the purview of the Code. Furthermore, even on matters within the Code's area of concern, the lawyer may have to look outside its provisions to federal and state laws on taxation, trade regulation, banking restrictions, and the like.

CHARACTERISTICS

Commercial law in the United States lacks two of the characteristics which distinguished the law merchant during the middle ages and which have been retained in many civil law countries. First, the separate commercial courts that once existed in England had declined in influence by the seventeenth century and never took root in the colonies; commercial matters have always been heard by the ordinary law courts in the United States. To a limited extent the functions of special commercial tribunals are performed by well established bodies, notably the American Arbitration Association, which offer facilities for com-

---

[24] The Code is divided into nine major substantive "articles" which correspond roughly to the "books" of a civil law code; these in turn are divided into "parts" which correspond to "titles"; and these are divided into "sections" which correspond to "articles."

[25] Courses entitled "commercial law" or "commercial transactions" have only recently begun to replace separate courses in such subjects as sales and negotiable instruments in American law schools.

[26] The Constitution gave Congress the power to establish "uniform laws on the subject of bankruptcies throughout the United States." The present act is the Bankruptcy Act of 1898, as amended. There are also assorted state laws concerning the rights of creditors against distressed debtors. Admiralty law is, for the most part, case law as laid down by the federal courts supplemented by a few federal statutes. Problems of federal jurisdiction form a peculiarly significant part of American admiralty law.

mercial arbitration. Second, the medieval conception of merchants as a distinct class for whom commercial law was specially designed also disappeared from English law before it had a chance to influence American law, and the concepts of "merchant" and "commercial act," found in many civil law countries, are virtually unknown in the United States. Bankruptcy, for example, is available to all persons and not just to merchants. The Uniform Commercial Code does include a definition of "merchant" in its article on the sale of goods and provides a few special rules which apply to such persons because of their expertise, but the Code as a whole applies to both merchants and non-merchants, and with these few exceptions it applies to both alike.

At the same time American commercial law produced some important developments of its own. In the field of negotiable instruments the almost universal habit of making significant payments by check has resulted in an elaborate body of case and statute law which is systematized by the Code. In sales law the seller's responsibility in breach of warranty for furnishing defective goods has been in the process of expansion for about a century, largely at the hands of the courts.[27] Where the claim is for personal injury, the issues are closely related to those of tort law and take on special importance because of the substantial recovery allowed by juries in such cases. The flexibility of commercial law is nowhere more evident than in its recognition and development of new legal devices to secure the extension of credit required for the distribution of goods ranging from automobiles to shoes, on both the wholesale and retail level; the conditional sale and the trust receipt[28] are leading examples. The most important single contribution of the Code is in consolidating, simplifying, and modernizing the law of such secured transactions in personal property.

On the whole, however, the Code, like the uniform laws which preceded it, represents no drastic upheaval in concepts and doctrines, but rather an effort to order the law and to bring it into harmony with current commercial practices. Nor does it make a complete break with the past, for like most of those uniform laws it provides that the "principles of law and equity,

[27] For an example, see fn. 12, p. 51 *supra*.

[28] The name "trust receipt" is misleading since this type of security device bears no relation to the concept of trust discussed at p. 91 *supra*.

including the law merchant . . . shall supplement its provisions" unless they are "displaced by the particular provisions" of the Code.[29] The draftsmen of the Code have also tried to allow for future change. In some instances they have purposely failed to provide for a problem to leave room for further development on a state-by-state basis;[30] in others the Code provisions expressly admit of change by developing usages. While the Code is intended to be a semi-permanent piece of legislation, it is hoped that it will be flexible enough to accommodate itself to future developments by both courts and legislatures.

SUGGESTED READINGS

The most useful work is the *Uniform Commercial Code* (1962 Official Text with Comments) itself. The Code, the most important of the prior uniform laws, and a student text with sample forms are contained in Braucher and Sutherland, *Commercial Transactions: Text—Forms—Statutes* (2nd ed. 1958). The Committee on Continuing Legal Education of the American Law Institute has published monographs explaining the principal articles of the Code. The standard work on sales, Williston, *The Law Governing Sales of Goods* (rev. ed. 1948), in four volumes with cumulative supplement, was published before the Code. Vold, *Handbook of the Law of Sales* (2nd ed. 1959) is a newer book which discusses the Code. Britton, *Handbook of the Law of Bills and Notes* (2nd ed. 1961) a recent volume on negotiable instruments, does not discuss the Code. The standard works on bankruptcy are MacLachlan, *Handbook of the Law of Bankruptcy* (1956), a single volume, and *Collier on Bankruptcy* (14th ed. by Moore), in nine loose-leaf volumes with current supplements. Two books on insurance are Patterson, *Essentials of Insurance Law* (2nd ed. 1957) and Vance, *Handbook on the Law of Insurance* (3rd ed. by Anderson 1951). The most recent volume on admiralty is Gilmore and Black, *The Law of Admiralty* (1957).

---

[29] This use of prior law to decide "omitted cases" is characteristic of a number of American statutes which have, in the main, codified existing case law.

[30] For example, the regulation of sales on credit to consumers in order to protect them from overreaching by sellers and financial institutions, is purposely left largely untouched by the Code and is now the subject of special retail installment sales acts recently enacted in most states.

BUSINESS ENTERPRISES

Scope and Sources

The most common forms for the more than ten million business enterprises in the United States are the individual proprietorship, the partnership, either general or limited, and the corporation.[31] The overwhelming majority are individual proprietorships; partnerships and corporations each account for less than ten percent of the total. Nevertheless, business corporations dominate the economy and employ three fourths of the labor force. In keeping with the fragmentation of American private law, what is here treated as the law of business enterprises is commonly regarded neither as part of a comprehensive body of commercial law nor as a unit in itself, but rather as such separate fields as agency, partnerships, and, most important, corporations.

Business enterprises are almost invariably organized under state law,[32] and incorporation has historically been regarded as founded upon a state grant.[33] When, after the Civil War, it became an established principle of constitutional law that no state could exclude a corporation incorporated in another state from engaging in interstate commerce within its territory, large corporations began to seek out the most favorable state of incorporation and some of the smaller states tailored their corporation laws to attract them. Delaware has been the most successful and leads all other states by a wide margin as the state of incorporation for large corporations. Differences among

[31] Less used forms of unincorporated business enterprise are the joint stock company or joint stock association in which ownership interests are represented by shares of stock, and the Massachusetts or business trust, in which the business is managed by trustees for the benefit of members. An informal undertaking to carry out a particular venture and dissolve upon its completion may be regarded as a joint venture or joint enterprise, with most of the characteristics of a partnership. Most jurisdictions distinguish between business and non-profit corporations with a separate statute for each. Municipalities, such as cities, towns, and villages, are commonly organized as municipal corporations under special state statutes. Corporations are also used by the federal and state governments as public entities to carry on some kinds of governmental activity.

[32] Some banking institutions, however, may be federally chartered and there are a few other exceptions.

[33] Until the beginning of the nineteenth century a corporation could only be formed pursuant to a special act of a state legislature, but by the end of the Civil War general state incorporation laws had been widely enacted and by the end of the century use of special legislative charters had been almost entirely abolished.

most state corporation laws are not fundamental, however, and although the American Bar Association's Model Business Corporation Act has been followed in a number of states, there has been no substantial demand for a uniform act or for federal control over the formation of corporations. Some of the chief statutory differences relate to the rights of shareholders to get money out of the corporation by the declaration of dividends, partial liquidations, and share purchases and redemptions, but the same results can be reached in most states even though procedures may vary. Case law doctrines have contributed to uniformity and, in spite of the large statutory ingredient, the courts have played a major role in such important and expanding areas of corporation law as the fiduciary duties owed by directors, officers, and shareholders. In addition, the corporate papers, such as the charter, by-laws, and resolutions of the shareholders and board of directors, are of great importance. There is considerably more uniformity in the field of partnerships as a result of the adoption by most states of the Uniform Partnership Act and the Uniform Limited Partnership Act. The law of agency is to be found largely in judicial decisions.

In recent decades the activities of business enterprises have been increasingly affected by federal law. Congress, under the commerce power, has regulated the interstate distribution and trading of securities by such statutes as the Securities Act of 1933 and the Securities and Exchange Act of 1934, which are administered by the Securities and Exchange Commission.[34] Taxation, trade regulation, and the regulation of particular industries have greatly affected business enterprises. The rules and decisions of the agencies that administer these laws are also an important source of law to the lawyer engaged in practice in this field.

CHARACTERISTICS

The corporation is the only one of the three principal forms of business enterprise that has traditionally been regarded for most legal purposes as an entity separate and apart from the persons who compose it. It may, of course, deal in property,

---

[34] The Commission is not empowered to decide whether a particular security may be issued to the public, but only to require full disclosure so that prospective investors can make an informed decision for themselves. Most states also have their own statutes regulating the sale of securities, which are popularly known as "blue sky laws."

make contracts, and sue and be sued, all in its corporate name, and a shareholder's risk is limited to his investment. It is true that modern statutes have departed from the older strict view that a partnership is an aggregate rather than an entity so that a partnership may have these and other characteristics of an entity.[35] And under special statutes a limited partnership may be created in which the risk of the limited or special partners, who take no part in management, is restricted to their capital contributions, although unlimited liability remains in the management group of partners.[36] But the corporation is the only one of these three forms in which existence may be perpetual,[37] in which ownership interests are readily transferable by the sale of stock, in which management is centralized in a board of directors, and which is treated as an entity for most federal and state tax purposes . Formation of a corporation to obtain these advantages involves formality and expense which are foreign to either of the other types of business enterprise. No formalities attend the creation of an individual proprietorship or even of a general partnership, which is viewed as a voluntary personal relationship arising from agreement among partners.[38]

In each state there is a single statute which applies generally to all business corporations regardless of size or distribution of ownership. Nevertheless, corporations vary greatly in structure and one of the current problems of corporation law is how best to take account of the obvious differences between the large publicly held, or "public" corporation and the small closely held, or "close," corporation. The law seems to have developed, for the most part, with the economically dominant public corporation in mind.[39]

One of the chief characteristics of the American corporation is the separation of management from ownership. Although

---

[35] There is also no upper limit to the number of partners in the United States.

[36] The limited partnership was first introduced in New York in 1822 by a statute patterned after the French *Code de Commerce* which authorizes the societé en comandite.

[37] An individual proprietorship terminates with the death of the proprietor and a partnership is technically dissolved by the death or withdrawal of a general partner.

[38] Statutes may require the filing of the name of an individual proprietorship or partnership. Since a limited partnership is purely a creature of statute, it must be organized in accordance with the formalities prescribed by statute.

[39] "One-man corporations," wholly owned by one person or by another corporation, are common, but most states still require at least three incorporators for the incorporation of such an enterprise and at least three directors for its management.

authority to make fundamental changes in character or organization, as by merger, dissolution, or amendment of the corporate charter, remains in the shareholders as owners of the corporation, the management of the corporation is entrusted to a separate group, the board of directors. The corporate officers, commonly president, vice-president, secretary, and treasurer, are appointed by the board of directors, as agents of the corporation charged with execution of the board's policies. The powers of the board of directors are derived from statute rather than from contract of shareholders and can be modified by agreement only within statutory limits. Typically it controls such matters as products, prices, labor relations, financing, and dividends. The directors are elected by the shareholders as their representatives and may in extreme cases be removed by them for cause.[40] They owe a fiduciary duty to all shareholders to act for the good of the corporation and not for their personal gain and they may be held accountable by even a minority interest for abuse of this duty.[41] But they are not agents of the shareholders and they are not subject to the demands of a majority of shareholders. Control of the board through election of directors can give effective control of the management of the corporation, and the election of directors is the principal function of the shareholders' annual meeting.

Shareholder control is difficult, however, in public corporations because of the dispersion of ownership.[42] The only practical way to exercise shareholder voting power and to meet substantial quorum requirements for shareholders' annual meetings is by proxy voting, through agents who are present to vote the shares of absent owners. This device favors perpetuation of existing management, which proposes its own nominees for directors. However, shares of American corporations are reg-

---

[40] Directors may or may not be officers and in most jurisdictions need not be shareholders. Unless they are also officers they are not usually compensated beyond their expenses, although the trend is toward paying directors' salaries.

[41] Although a shareholder cannot sue in his own name to enforce corporate rights, he may, subject to some limitations, maintain what is known as a derivative suit, equitable in nature, on behalf of the corporation if the directors wrongfully fail to enforce a corporate claim against persons either within or without the corporation. In some instances a shareholder may also bring a direct individual suit in his own name against the corporation to enforce his own interest.

[42] It has been estimated that more than fifteen million Americans own stock. The largest American corporation, American Telephone and Telegraph Company, has some two million shareholders.

istered on the corporate books,[43] and shareholders who seek to overthrow management are entitled to inspect the stock book and obtain a list of names and addresses of all shareholders in order to solicit proxy votes in a "proxy fight." Solicitation of proxies in most major corporations is subject to the rules of the Securities and Exchange Commission, which also requires detailed financial statements that shareholders may use to evaluate management.[44]

SUGGESTED READINGS

The most recent of a number of one-volume texts on corporations and related fields is Henn, *Handbook of the Law of Corporations and Other Business Enterprises* (1961). Others are *Ballantine on Corporations* (rev. ed. 1946); Lattin, *The Law of Corporations* (1959); and Stevens, *Handbook on the Law of Private Corporations* (2nd ed. 1949). Longer works are the *Model Business Corporation Act Annotated* (1960), in three volumes with current pocket supplements; Hornstein, *Corporation Law and Practice* (1959), in two volumes with current pocket supplements; and Fletcher, *Cyclopedia of the Law of Private Corporations* (perm. ed. 1931-62), in twenty periodically revised volumes with current pocket supplements. Two works on the financial aspects of corporations are Dewing, *The Financial Policy of Corporations* (5th ed. 1953), in two volumes, and Guthmann and Dougall, *Corporate Financial Policy* (3rd ed. 1955). The standard treatise on the regulation of securities is Loss, *Securities Regulation* (2nd ed. 1961), in three volumes with current pocket supplements. A one volume text on partnerships is Crane, *Handbook on the Law of Partnership and Other Unincorporated Associations* (2nd ed. 1952). The best work on agency is the *Restatement of Agency, Second* (1958). One volume texts are Seavey, *Studies in Agency* (1949), by the reporter for the *Re-*

[43] Shares of stock may be of various classes with different dividend and voting rights and may be either common or preferred. They evidence an ownership interest, often called an "equity" because of the equitable nature of the shareholder's derivative suit, and must be distinguished from debt securities such as bonds. While bonds are typically issued in bearer form, shares of stock are not. Transfer of investment securities, debt as well as equity, is governed in many states by the Uniform Commercial Code, which replaces the Uniform Stock Transfer Act.

[44] While, except for the regulated industries, the government does not formally prescribe auditing and accounting standards, the Commission has had considerable influence in raising these standards in public corporations to a very high level. There is, however, no individual or group which supervises the management of the corporation on the shareholders' behalf.

statement of Agency, Second; Ferson, *Principles of Agency* (1954); and Mechem, *Outlines of the Law of Agency* (4th ed. by P. Mechem 1952).

Chapter XII

Public Law

The principal fields of public law in the United States are constitutional law, administrative law, trade regulation, labor law, tax law, and criminal law. What is their purview, how have they developed, and what are their distinctive features?

CONSTITUTIONAL LAW

SCOPE AND SOURCES

The study of constitutional law, as that term is used in the United States, is chiefly the study of those decisions of the Supreme Court of the United States that have interpreted the federal Constitution. This excludes some questions of constitutional intepretation which the Court has declined to entertain on the ground that they are "political questions," for the executive or legislature to resolve, and therefore not justiciable. It also excludes the large number of Supreme Court decisions which turn on other than constitutional grounds. Although each of the states has its own written constitution, "constitutional law" is ordinarily taken to mean federal rather than state constitutional law.

The primary source in this field is, of course, the Constitution itself, the oldest written national constitution now in use.[1] Less than eight thousand words in length, it has been able to survive with relatively little amendment because important terms

---

[1] Among the aids in its interpretation are the records of the Constitutional Convention and a series of essays entitled *The Federalist*, written by three of its framers, Hamilton, Madison, and Jay, during the contest over its ratification in New York. But the Court in construing the Constitution has not usually felt bound by the intention of its framers, in the same way as it would if it were construing a statute.

such as "commerce," "necessary and proper," "due process," and "full faith and credit," are sufficiently laconic to allow for adaptation. In Chief Justice Marshall's words, the nature of a constitution requires "that only its great outlines should be marked, its important objects designated, and the minor ingredients which compose these objects be deduced from the nature of the objects themselves. . . . We must never forget, that it is a *constitution* we are expounding."[2]

CHARACTERISTICS

One of the cardinal limitations on the Court's power of judicial review of federal and state legislation on constitutional grounds is that it will decide only a ripened controversy in which the results are of immediate consequence to the parties and will not render advisory opinions or entertain non-adversary proceedings. One writer has called it the "central paradox" of the jurisdiction and function of the Supreme Court that "its special role is to resolve questions of general importance transcending the interests of the litigants and yet it will do so only where necessary to adjudicate a conventional legal dispute between the parties."[3] Among the other significant restraints which the Court imposes upon itself are "never to anticipate a question of constitutional law in advance of the necessity of deciding it" and "never to formulate a rule of constitutional law broader than is required by the precise facts to which it is to be applied."[4] If the Court can base its decision on some ground other than a constitutional one, it will do so; if it can dismiss an appeal on constitutional grounds from a state court of last resort by finding that the judgment rested on an independent ground under state law, it will do so. All in all, the mechanics of judicial review tend to bring constitutional issues before the Court, not at times of its own choosing, but at times determined by aggrieved litigants and by history. Most of these issues can be grouped under two main headings: maintenance of the federal system and preservation of individual rights.

The major problems under the first heading arise under the commerce clause. To ensure a free national market, the framers of the Constitution entrusted to Congress the power

---

[2] *McCulloch* v. *Maryland*, 17 U.S. (4 Wheat) 316 (1819).

[3] Freund, *The Supreme Court of the United States* 16 (1961).

[4] *Liverpool, New York & Philadelphia SS. Co.* v. *Commissioners of Emigration*, 113 U.S. 33, 39 (1885).

"To regulate Commerce with foreign Nations, and among the several States, and with the Indian Tribes."[5] Congress was slow to exercise this power until an industrial society emerged after the Civil War, and it was not until the challenge to the New Deal legislation enacted during the administration of President Franklin Delano Roosevelt that the Court, in the late 1930's, departed from earlier doctrine and finally gave the clause the broad reading which it has today. The commerce power, along with the taxing and spending powers, has given Congress its present wide role in national economic life. Under its authority to regulate business and labor when engaged in production for interstate commerce, Congress has laid the foundations of such burgeoning fields as trade regulation and labor law.

In addition to its positive aspect, as a source of federal power, the clause has a negative aspect, as a limitation on state power. It is, of course, clear that a state statute must yield if it conflicts with a federal statute enacted under the clause, and an act of Congress that "occupies" a particular field supersedes all state legislation in that field. But beyond this, it was early established that even in the absence of federal statute, state legislation was unconstitutional if it improperly burdened or discriminated against interstate commerce. The clause is thus an important limitation upon exercise by the states of their tax and police powers, both of which may have an impact upon interstate commerce. But although it has been second only to the Fourteenth Amendment as a basis of judicial review of the exercise of state power, no precise line can be drawn between proper and improper state legislation affecting interstate commerce.

The second main heading, preservation of individual rights, derives chiefly from the amendments to the Constitution. The Bill of Rights, embodied in the first ten amendments ratified in 1791, secures the rights of the individual against the federal government. Of even greater significance are the protections which the federal Constitution affords the individual against the states.[6] The chief source of these is the Fourteenth Amendment, the most important of three amendments to the Constitution adopted soon after the Civil War and originally intended

---

[5] The Articles of Confederation had given Congress no power over interstate or foreign commerce and each of the thirteen original states had been free to erect trade barriers at the expense of its neighbors.

[6] There are also, to be sure, protections in all of the state constitutions.

to abolish slavery and ensure the freedom of the Negro. Its principal clauses provide that no state shall "deprive any person of life, liberty, or property, without due process of law," and that no state shall "deny to any person within its jurisdiction the equal protection of the laws." "Due process," now the most prestigious of constitutional doctrines, was originally regarded principally as a guaranty of fair procedure. By the end of the nineteenth century, however, the Supreme Court had expanded the concept to impose a restriction on the substantive reasonableness of legislation enacted by the states under their police power, as their power to provide for the public welfare is called. It entered a period in which the chief use of the due process clause was to strike down state statutes as unconstitutional invasions of property rights, including those of corporations as well as individuals.[7]

Since the late 1930's, however, these cases have declined in significance in the face of the use of the due process clause for the protection of civil liberties. The Court has now made clear that the most fundamental, although not all, of the more detailed protections afforded against the federal government by the Bill of Rights, are to be read into the more laconic due process clause of the Fourteenth Amendment. The protections of freedom of speech, assembly, press, and religious worship, the prohibition of establishment of a state religion, and some of the procedural safeguards for criminal cases are among those which have been held to be incorporated. Even more recently the Court, under the equal protection clause, has extended the rights of minority groups by forbidding racial segregation by the states in public schools and other public facilities. It should be noted, however, that the Constitution protects the individual against governmental action only and not against the acts of private individuals.

SUGGESTED READINGS

There is no current standard treatise on constitutional law. There is, however, no shortage of monographs on related subjects. Two of the best are Freund, *The Supreme Court of the United States* (1961), an introduction to the business, purposes, and performance of the Court, and Gellhorn, *American Rights*:

---

[7] The Court had also determined that corporations were "persons" entitled to the protections of the Fourteenth Amendment.

The Constitution in Action (1960), an introduction to the protection of individual rights based on lectures originally intended for foreign law students. Mason and Beaney, *The Supreme Court in a Free Society* (1959), and Beth, *Politics, the Constitution and the Supreme Court* (1962) are short elementary textbooks. A section by section analysis of the Constitution and its amendments can be found in Corwin, *The Constitution and What It Means Today* (12th ed. 1958) or in Corwin and Peltason, *Understanding the Constitution* (rev. ed. 1958). Schwartz, *American Constitutional Law* (1955), is a one-volume introduction intended for English readers. For an annotated edition of the Constitution, see Corwin (editor), *The Constitution of the United States: Analysis and Interpretation* (1953). The constitutions of the United States and of the states are collected in two volumes entitled *Constitutions of the United States: National and State* (1962), prepared by the Legislative Drafting Research Fund of Columbia University.

ADMINISTRATIVE LAW

Scope and Sources

Administrative law is concerned with the powers and procedures of those organs of government, other than legislatures and courts, that affect private interests either by rule or by decision.[8] The field is relatively young and is still in the stage of rapid development. It is heavily procedural in its emphasis and does not include the substantive law created by administrative agencies. It deals chiefly though not exclusively with the discharge by public officials of functions related to rule-making and adjudication,[9] and focuses on control of administrators by the courts. Although administrative agencies abound on the state and local levels, the federal agencies have widest impact and are the easiest to describe.

The administrative process on the federal level goes back as far as 1789, but its modern origins date from the establishment in 1887 of the Interstate Commerce Commission to deal

---

[8] Such an organ of government, commonly called an agency, may also be known by such names as administrator, authority, board, bureau, commission, department, division, or office.

[9] The discharge by public officials of functions unrelated to rule-making or adjudication is included in the subject of public administration, a part of the field of political science, which is not taught in American law schools.

with the problems of the railroad industry. The Commission set the pattern for those independent regulatory agencies—functioning outside of the executive departments and regulating some aspect of private activity—which are the most distinctive species of administrative body in the United States. Federal administrative agencies of all kinds multiplied rapidly under New Deal legislation enacted in the 1930's during the administration of President Roosevelt.[10] There are now some hundred and twenty federal agencies, with such diverse concerns as airlines, atomic energy, banking, farm prices, immigration, labor relations, and old age pensions.

Administrative law is compounded of constitutional law, statutes, case law, and agency rules and decisions. On the constitutional plane, the effect of the due process clause upon administrative procedure is of chief importance. Most significant on the statutory level is the Federal Administrative Procedure Act of 1946, which sought to regularize administrative procedure and to clarify the scope of judicial review of administrative action. Case law also plays a surprisingly large role, due in part to the general nature of many of the constitutional and statutory directives. Because there is no separate system of courts which dispense administrative law, its judicially developed principles are similar to those of other fields.

CHARACTERISTICS

Agency procedures may be formal or informal. The vast bulk of decisions are reached by informal proceedings with nothing resembling a formal hearing. As for the small fraction of cases where formal proceedings are had, the variety of agencies and the scope of their activities defy both general description and uniform regulation. Although the Federal Administrative Procedure Act lays down general guidelines of procedure on matters common to most agencies, no comprehensive and detailed procedural code has been deemed feasible. Nevertheless, the dominant theme of the due process clause of the federal Constitution runs throughout administrative procedure.[11] The

---

10 Some of the better known examples, in addition to the Interstate Commerce Commission, are the Federal Trade Commission, the National Labor Relations Board, and the Securities and Exchange Commission, all of which are discussed elsewhere.

11 State and local administrative agencies are also affected by due process requirements in state constitutions.

chief requirements of procedural due process are notice and an opportunity to have a fair hearing. While it is difficult to generalize and the rules in this area have evolved largely on an *ad hoc* basis through case law against the background of vague constitutional and statutory requirements, there is a growing view that a person is entitled to notice and a hearing analogous to a trial on disputed facts involved in an adjudication of his rights.[12] Hearings are commonly held before agency employees known as hearing examiners, whose initial findings are subject to the final decision of the agency. Notice to the person affected is characteristically brief and its contents are less important than the pleadings in court procedure. The procedure and rules of evidence for court hearings are not applicable and the emphasis on written evidence is great. A party affected by rule-making proceedings may also have the opportunity to present his case, but not ordinarily in a trial type of hearing.

Of the relatively small number of cases which go to formal administrative proceedings, an even smaller number is subjected to judicial review. Nevertheless, the judicial control of administrative actions is one of the most significant topics of American administrative law.[13] Because there is no special system of courts to handle administrative matters, judicial review is carried out within the framework created for conventional litigation in the regular courts. Most federal regulatory statutes specifically authorize review of particular actions of the agency charged with their administration.[14] Review is commonly appellate in nature, before a federal court of appeals on the record below; less often it is by an original action in a federal district court. Furthermore, there is a general statutory authorization of review in the Federal Administrative Procedure Act[15] as well as non-statutory review in some cases.[16] Review may also possible under

---

[12] The area of license revocation has been especially troublesome, and a licensee's right to a hearing on the revocation of his license may turn on whether the particular license is regarded as conferring upon him a "right," or merely a "privilege."

[13] A justice of the Supreme Court of the United States has calculated that, "Review of administrative action, mainly reflecting enforcement of federal regulatory statutes, constitutes the largest category of the Court's work, comprising one-third of the total cases decided on the merits." Frankfurter, *The Supreme Court in the Mirror of Justices*, 105 U. Pa. L. Rev. 781, 793 (1957).

[14] This is also true of many state statutes.

[15] There is a similar provision in the Model State Administrative Procedure Act.

[16] This may be, *inter alia*, by injunction or declaratory judgment, or by the prerogative writs, which include mandamus, habeas corpus, and prohibition.

other circumstances, as when agency action requires court enforcement. A variety of doctrines tend to limit review of administrative adjudication to those who are immediately affected by a final order in a ripe controversy and have exhausted their administrative remedies. Full review can generally be had on the "law," but the "facts" will ordinarily be reviewed only to the extent of determining whether the administrative finding is supported by "substantial evidence," a scope of review which is similar to that applied to a finding of fact by a jury.

Administrative agencies, in spite of their considerable independence, are also subject to some control by the legislative and executive branches. Although there is no general provision for congressional review of administrative rules and regulations,[17] Congress has not hesitated to intervene in agency affairs through its control over agency budgets and through investigation by congressional committees. The President has the power, subject to the consent of the Senate, to appoint agency heads, but his power of removal before the end of a fixed term is severely circumscribed. He also controls the agencies' requests to Congress for funds, and has limited powers of reorganization of administrative agencies. Among the current concerns of Congress and the President is the tendency of those agencies which specialize in the regulation of a single industry to become "industry oriented" and assume the role of a partner rather than a governor of the affected industry. Criticism has also been directed at the combination in the same agency of the functions of legislating, investigating, initiating proceedings, and judging. This has been met in part by the division of functions within the agencies themselves and through increased independence for the hearing examiner.[18]

SUGGESTED READINGS

The leading treatise is Davis, *Administrative Law Treatise* (1958), in four volumes with current pocket supplements, and the most widely used one volume text is by the same author, Davis, *Administrative Law Text* (1959). Other texts are Parker,

---

[17] Some states have general procedures of this kind and Congress has made selective use of review in special circumstances.

[18] In one notable instance, that of the National Labor Relations Board, the function of initiating proceedings has been completely separated from the agency by the creation of an independent office of General Counsel with final authority to investigate and prosecute unfair labor practices.

Administrative Law (1952), and Schwartz, *An Introduction to American Administrative Law* (2nd ed. 1962), a book designed in part for British readers. Much helpful commentary can be found in Gellhorn and Byse, *Cases and Comments on Administrative Law* (1960), a casebook. A description of federal administrative agencies is contained in the *United States Government Organization Manual,* published annually.

TRADE REGULATION

SCOPE AND SOURCES

The field of trade regulation includes the law of antitrust, which is designed to encourage competition through the prevention of monopolization and the limitation of restraints of trade, and the law of unfair competition, which requires that competition meet acceptable standards of fairness. It may be defined to include the law of trade marks and trade names as well as the primarily statutory law of patents, and copyrights.[19] Although some regulation of trade was effected by case law before modern legislation, the principal sources today are federal, and to a lesser extent state,[20] statutes. Among the most significant of these are the three major antitrust statutes enacted by Congress for the purpose of promoting competition in interstate commerce.

The first and most important was the Sherman Antitrust Act, enacted in 1890 during the period of industrial expansion and concentration of economic power which followed the Civil War.[21] It prohibits in general terms unreasonable restraints of trade and monopolization. The Clayton Act, which followed in 1914, is somewhat more specific. With some exceptions, it pro-

---

[19] Patents are granted and copyrights are protected in accordance with federal statutes enacted under an express constitutional provision. Trade marks and trade names are protected primarily by common law doctrines, buttressed by federal and state statute.

[20] State statutes include fair trade acts, widely enacted under an enabling clause in the federal antitrust laws, to permit "vertical" resale price-fixing agreements. Although antitrust statutes have also been enacted by most states, they have been effective in only a few.

[21]. The antitrust laws were named after the nineteenth-century "trust," a closely knit business combination, composed of many corporations in a single industry such as oil or sugar, and held together by a trust agreement under unified management by a board of trustees.

hibits: first, exclusive dealing, tying arrangements,[22] and similar restrictions on the distribution of goods; second, price discrimination, or differentiation, between purchasers, as well as certain related discriminatory practices;[23] and third, acquisition by one corporation of stock or assets of another corporation— where the effect of any of these "may be substantially to lessen competition or to tend to create a monopoly." While the Sherman Act condemns only existing evils, the Clayton Act requires merely a reasonable probability that these evils will result. The third major statute, the Federal Trade Commission Act, also enacted in 1914, is directed generally at "unfair methods of competition." It created the Federal Trade Commission, which is empowered to enforce the Act.[24] Together, these three statutes affect the "horizontal" relationships of a business with its competitors, the "vertical" relationships of a business with its suppliers and customers, and in some cases the internal corporate relationship within the business enterprise itself.

Because virtually all of American business is privately owned and managed, the maintenance and control of competition is of the greatest importance. In some fields, however, Congress has departed from the ideal of free competition. Thus, there are limited exemptions from the antitrust laws for such industries as aviation, communications, railroads, trucking, and shipping, all of which are closely supervised by special regulatory agencies. Also exempted in most of their activities are labor unions and agricultural cooperatives, which have peculiar problems.

CHARACTERISTICS

A major characteristic of the field of antitrust is that many of the statutory provisions, and particularly those of the Sherman Act, are couched in broader and more general terms than is customary for legislation in the United States. This calculated imprecision has given a decisive role to the judiciary, which has been responsible for interpreting the statutes and adapting them

---

22 An exclusive dealing arrangement is one in which one firm is allowed to obtain the product of another on condition that it will not deal in the competing products of third parties. A tying arrangement involves a sale or lease of a product on condition that some other product be purchased with it.

23 This second prohibition is contained in the Robinson-Patman Act of 1936, which amends and is now a part of the Clayton Act.

24 The Federal Trade Commission Act also has jurisdiction over such unfair trade practices as false and misleading advertising, and over misbranding and related practices in connection with food, drugs, and cosmetics.

to the changing patterns of production and distribution that have evolved since their passage. Rather than lay down precise and inflexible rules, the courts too have employed a general "rule of reason," or standard of reasonableness, in implementing some of the statutory mandates. Its application has varied from time to time and from industry to industry according to the circumstances as judges have struggled with economic data in order to accomplish the objectives of the governing statutes. There is thus no absolute limit to the size of a business enterprise and size alone, or even dominance, is not of itself condemned, although these are among the circumstances to be evaluated. The courts are in agreement, however, that some practices, such as "horizontal" arrangements among competitors to affect prices or divide markets, are so offensive as to be *per se* unreasonable. Doctrines more similar to *per se* rules than to a "rule of reason" are also applied to exclusive dealing and tying arrangements under the Clayton Act and to most forms of price discrimination. As might be expected, there has been considerable controversy over the proper domain of the rule of reason and of *per se* unreasonableness under all the antitrust statutes.

Another of the salient features of the antitrust laws is the unique panoply of remedies available for their enforcement. The government may proceed against violations in three principal ways: first, by a civil proceeding of an equitable nature brought by the Justice Department to enjoin violations of the Sherman and Clayton Acts; second, by a criminal prosecution also brought by the Justice Department for a more limited class of violations, largely under the Sherman Act, which are punishable by fine and imprisonment; and third, by administrative proceedings brought by the Federal Trade Commission under the Clayton and Federal Trade Commission Acts and leading to a cease-and-desist order by the Commission, appealable to a federal court of appeals and carrying a fine as the sanction for violation. In a majority of civil proceedings a settlement is negotiated between the defendant and the government before trial and a consent decree is entered by the court.[25] Whether entered with consent or not, the decree may be broadly phrased to end violations and to prevent future resumptions, and may

---

[25] One inducement to the defendant is that consent decrees are an exception to the general rule of the Clayton Act that a judgment or decree establishing a violation of the antitrust laws in a proceeding brought by the government is prima facie evidence of violation in a later civil suit by a private party.

even require dissolution of an offending enterprise or divestiture of its holdings. Remedies are also given to private parties, the most important being the treble damage action under the Sherman and Clayton Acts, in which the aggrieved party may be awarded three times the amount of damages that he proves. Trade mark, copyright, and patent rights are enforced exclusively by private civil suits. Complaints by private parties are also responsible for many of the actions brought by the government under the antitrust laws and by the Federal Trade Commission to prevent unfair trade practices.

One of the criticisms of the laws has been the overlapping of functions of the Justice Department and the Federal Trade Commission, notably under the Clayton Act.[26] While in general they do not conduct simultaneous proceedings and seek to avoid conflict, their approach to antitrust problems will not always be the same since the Justice Department, as an arm of the executive, more closely reflects the view of the administration than does the independent Commission. Because of the fluidity of the law, both have considerable discretion and both have substantially influenced its development. Their enforcement has, on the whole, been effective in preserving competition, notwithstanding the fact that the American economic system revolves around a relatively few very large industrial corporations.[27]

SUGGESTED READINGS

A college textbook on government regulation of business, including antitrust, unfair trade practices, regulated industries, and public enterprises, is Wilcox, *Public Policies Toward Business* (rev. ed. 1960). Dewey, *Monopoly in Economics and Law* (1959) is a text on the economic and legal aspects of antitrust. Van Cise, *Understanding the Antitrust Laws* (1958) is an introductory booklet for practicing lawyers. The *Report of the Attorney General's National Committee to Study the Antitrust Laws* (1955) analyzes the antitrust laws and gives criticisms and suggestions for change. The only treatise in the field is Toulmin, *A Treatise on the Anti-Trust Laws of the United States*

---

26 Violations of the Sherman Act, under the jurisdiction of the Justice Department, may also amount to violations of the Federal Trade Commission Act, under the jurisdiction of the Commission.

27 It has been calculated that some 140 corporations own 45% of the industrial assets of the United States. Adelman, *The Measurement of Industrial Concentration,* 33 Review of Economics and Statistics 269, 289 (1951).

(1949), in seven volumes with current pocket supplements. Handler, *Antitrust in Perspective* (1957) is a monograph based on three lectures. Works on patents include Toulmin, *Handbook of Patents* (2nd ed. 1954), a one-volume treatise, and *Walker on Patents* (Deller's ed. 1937), in four volumes with current cumulative supplement. Works on copyrights include Ball, *The Law of Copyright and Literary Property* (1944), a one-volume treatise, and *Howell's Copyright Law* (rev. ed. by Latman 1962), a smaller volume.

LABOR LAW

Scope and Sources

Labor law, in its broadest sense, is the law that affects working persons by virtue of their employment relationship, a relationship which in the United States is ordinarily with a private employer. One branch of the field deals with the welfare of workers as individuals. It includes such common state statutes as those establishing workmen's compensation, prescribing wage and hour standards, preventing harmful child labor, protecting women workers, and proscribing discrimination in employment on the grounds of race, religion, or national origin. There is a federal wage and hour law, the Fair Labor Standards Act of 1938, which provides for minimum wages, maximum hours beyond which additional compensation for overtime is payable, and the prohibition of child labor.[28] There is also a federal con-

---

[28] Statutes in these areas suffered at first from attacks on their constitutionality, and their history provides a good example of the interplay of the legislative and judicial branches in the American constitutional system. The first federal child labor law was enacted in 1916, but in 1918 the Supreme Court, five judges to four, declared it to be unconstitutional as beyond the power of Congress under the commerce clause. *Hammer* v. *Dagenhart*, 247 U. S. 251 (1918). Congress enacted a second law in 1919 under its power to tax, but in 1922 it was again held by the Supreme Court, with only one dissenting vote, to have exceeded its power. *Bailey* v. *Drexel Furniture Co.* (*Child Labor Tax Case*), 259 U. S. 20 (1922). In 1924 Congress proposed an amendment to the Constitution to enable it to enact a child labor law, but it had not been ratified by the necessary three fourths of the states by the time of the passage of the Fair Labor Standards Act in 1938. That act was held constitutional in *United States* v. *Darby*, 312 U. S. 100 (1941), in which the court by a unanimous vote expressly overruled *Hammer* v. *Dagenhart*. State, as distinguished from federal, minimum wage laws also ran into constitutional difficulties, in their case under the due process clause of the Fourteenth Amendment, until the Supreme Court, in a five to four vote, upheld the Washington state minimum wage law in *West Coast Hotel* v. *Parrish*, 300 U. S. 379 (1937), expressly overruling an earlier decision.

tributory social security system which provides an old age retirement annuity, payments to survivors, and related benefits. Unemployment insurance is provided in all states by a cooperative federal-state plan.

The second major division of the field deals with disputes arising out of the activities of organized labor, and it is this subject, sometimes called labor relations, with which American labor law is chiefly concerned. Its modern development began in the 1930's. Prior to that time, the law of labor relations was largely case law, based on precedent and traditional principles, and generally favorable to employers, who were able to obtain court injunctions forbidding many forms of union activity. In reaction to judicial excesses, the role of the courts was severely circumscribed by statute. The Norris-LaGuardia Act of 1932 so curtailed the power of the federal courts to issue injunctions in labor disputes that it is now almost impossible for an employer to get an injunction against peaceful labor activity.[29] The first comprehensive labor relations statute came soon afterward with the enactment in 1935 of the National Labor Relations Act, commonly known as the Wagner Act, to promote collective bargaining between employers and unions.[30] It assured employees of the right to organize and to bargain collectively, and proscribed a list of unfair labor practices by employers, including discrimination against employees because of their union activity and refusal to bargain with an authorized collective bargaining agent. It created the National Labor Relations Board and gave it two tasks: first, to conduct elections in which employees can, if they choose, select representatives for bargaining purposes; and second, to hear and determine charges of unfair labor practices, subject to review by a federal court of appeals. The Board may also seek a court injunction against such practices. In 1947, a

---

[29] Within a few years many of the states had enacted similar anti-injunction statutes.

[30] The National Industrial Recovery Act of 1933 had recognized the right of employees to bargain collectively, but that statute was held unconstitutional by a unanimous vote in *Schechter Poultry Corp.* v. *United States*, 295 U. S. 495 (1935). The *Schechter* case is notable as one of only two cases in which the Supreme Court has invalidated an attempted congressional delegation of lawmaking power to an administrative agency. The constitutionality of the Wagner Act as a valid exercise of the commerce clause was upheld by a five to four decision in *National Labor Relations Board* v. *Jones & Laughlin Steel Corp.*, 301 U. S. 1 (1937). A minority of states also have labor relations laws which are generally applicable only to small businesses that have no substantial impact on commerce and therefore do not come under federal legislation.

climate of public opinion less favorable to labor resulted in the enactment over a presidential veto of the Labor Management Relations Act, popularly known as the Taft-Hartley Act. Among its most important provisions were those establishing for the first time unfair labor practices on behalf of unions, including coercion and certain secondary labor activity in which pressures are applied beyond the immediate parties to a labor dispute. It also limited agreements between an employer and a union requiring or encouraging employees to be members of the union.[31] The most recent major enactment is the Labor-Management Reporting and Disclosure Act of 1959, also known as the Landrum-Griffin Act, which amends the two earlier enactments in various respects and provides for the regulation of internal union affairs to ensure honesty and fairness to individual members.

Characteristics

In the three decades since the first modern labor legislation, union membership has grown sixfold. Although it still comprises only about one third of the non-agricultural work force, leaving most industrial enterprises without union representation, many of the characteristics of American labor law can be ascribed to the distinctive features of organized labor.[32] One of the most significant of these is its lack of political orientation. Organized labor's chief goals have been better wages and working conditions rather than general social reform, and while it has not hesitated to support specific legislation and particular candidates, it has neither maintained its own political party nor permanently allied itself with either of the two major parties. It has achieved its objectives primarily through collectively negotiated agree-

---

[31] The "closed shop," in which union membership is required before a worker can be employed, is prohibited. The "union shop," in which a worker must join the union after he is hired, is generally permissible under federal law, but may be prohibited under "right-to-work" laws enacted in a minority of states under express provision in federal law that a stricter state law may supersede a federal law in this regard.

[32] Organized labor shows the pluralism that is so often characteristic of American institutions. While most union members belong to unions that are affiliated with the American Federation of Labor-Congress of Industrial Organizations (AFL-CIO), power is lodged in the many international unions which represent particular crafts and industries. Their local chapters are composed of employees in a particular geographical area or perhaps even a single factory, and it is the international union and not the federation, the AFL-CIO, with which the individual worker has his dealings.

ments with employers rather than by comprehensive legislation. These agreements both supplement minimum statutory benefits relating to wages, hours, and pensions, and add benefits which have no counterparts in case law or statute, such as paid vacations, sick leave, seniority, severance pay, and employee participation in the settlement of grievances. The peculiar significance of the collective bargaining agreement is symptomatic of the overall importance of voluntary private procedures for settlement of labor problems in the United States.

The labor relations laws themselves provide no significant governmental machinery for the settlement of disputes over employment conditions, but attempt only to compel bargaining in good faith between management and the elected union representatives of an appropriate bargaining unit of workers. Under the principle of majority rule, the representatives chosen by the majority are the exclusive bargaining agents for the entire unit. If the union is unable to negotiate a satisfactory collective bargaining agreement, the workers are free to strike upon the termination of any prior collective bargaining agreement, and it is this weapon that makes the bargaining process effective.[33] In order to avoid and shorten strikes, both federal and state governments provide mediation and conciliation facilities, but they can not force terms upon the parties.[34] Whether a strike is had or not, the end result of bargaining is a lengthy and detailed collective bargaining agreement between the employer and the union for a period, commonly of two years, during which the union ordinarily agrees not to strike. One of the key provisions will detail the procedures for the private settlement of employee grievances between the employer and representatives of the union, who act on behalf of the workers. Arbitration by an expert or a panel of experts is almost invariably provided as a last resort

---

[33] The proportion of man hours lost annually because of strikes is nevertheless very small, usually under one quarter of one per cent. The Taft-Hartley Act limits the right to strike in those rare cases where the strike would be a threat to the national health or safety, by providing for an 80-day injunction, to be obtained by the government, on the expiration of which the workers are again free to strike. Even here, the main reliance is on informal procedures. There are also limitations on the right of railroad and airline employees to strike under the Railway Labor Act. Strikes by federal government employees are prohibited by federal statute; state and municipal employees have been regularly held to lack the right to strike and a number of states have statutory provisions as well.

[34] Arbitration is rarely used to fix contract terms and federal law makes no provision for compulsory arbitration of labor disputes in private industry.

in the settlement of grievances and is especially desirable because of the absence of special labor courts. Should one of the parties refuse to observe an arbitration agreement, a court will order its specific performance, but it is a rare instance in which this extreme sanction is necessary. For the most part, although the collective bargaining agreement is a legally enforceable contract, its enforcement is entrusted to private agencies, with very limited reliance upon the courts.

Suggested Readings

There is no standard treatise in the field of labor law. Gregory, *Labor and the Law* (2nd rev. ed. with 1961 supp.) is a one-volume general introduction to labor relations. *The Guidebook to Labor Relations*, published annually by the Commerce Clearing House, gives a brief summary of the same field. A survey of labor laws of all kinds, with emphasis on state law, is contained in *Growth of Labor Law in the United States* (1962), a booklet published by the United States Department of Labor.

TAX LAW

Scope and Sources

The principal sources of federal revenue are individual income taxes, which make up well over one half; corporate income taxes, which contribute about one quarter; and excise taxes, which contribute about one sixth.[35] Customs receipts, which were once the mainstay of the federal tax system, and estate and gift taxes are now relatively insignificant sources. State and local authorities collect a considerably smaller amount than the federal government, chiefly through sales, income, and property taxes.[36] It is therefore not surprising that tax law in the United States is thought of largely in terms of the law of federal income taxation, which dwarfs all other devices for the raising of revenue and which has come to affect every other branch of the law. Federal estate and gift taxes also command attention, not because of their contribution to the national

---

[35]. Most of the rest results from a payroll tax which is used to support the social security system.

[36] A state payroll tax raises a substantial sum for unemployment insurance. State death and gift taxes contribute a relatively small amount.

coffers, but because of their impact upon the management of personal wealth.

The federal income tax has only recently atttained this importance. In 1895 the Supreme Court of the United States held that a federal tax on income was unconstitutional,[37] and it was not until 1913, when the Sixteenth Amendment to the Constitution became effective, that Congress was empowered "to lay and collect taxes on incomes." Although a progressive income tax on individuals was used in the 1930's during the New Deal to help reduce the extremes of wealth and poverty, as late as 1939 only one out of every twenty-five Americans of working age was a federal income taxpayer. All this changed with the Second World War, when the income tax became the dominant instrument for raising federal revenue, and today some fifty million taxable returns are filed annually.

The primary source of the law of federal income taxation is the Internal Revenue Code of 1954, which, with its amendments, contains all of the currently applicable federal revenue provisions except those relating to customs duties. Tax law is thus fundamentally statutory, and, although some of its areas have been greatly influenced by judicially developed doctrines, there is no other field in which statute law stands out above the decisions of the courts as such a definitive source of law. Treasury Regulations, promulgated by authority of the Secretary of the Treasury, lay down addition and detailed rules, intended to interpret, to implement, and to fill gaps in the Code. They are valid, however, only to the extent that they are not inconsistent with the Code. The most significant of the other administrative pronouncements are the published rulings of the Internal Revenue Service on stated sets of facts usually involving a problem common to a number of taxpayers.[38]

CHARACTERISTICS

While it is to the credit of the American taxpayer that he voluntarily reports his income and pays his taxes with commend-

---

[37] The Court's decision was based on a provision in the Constitution which forbade the federal government to levy a "direct Tax," unless apportioned among the states according to population. *Pollock* v. *Farmers' Loan & Trust Co.*, 157 U. S. 429 (1895), upheld on rehearing, 158 U. S. 601 (1895).

[38] Both Treasury Regulations and current rulings of the Internal Revenue Service are binding upon officials of the Service, and even the latter are often persuasive in court.

able responsibility and accuracy, the system would not function as well as it does without its extensive enforcement machinery. Primary responsibility for the administration of the tax laws is with the Internal Revenue Service, headed by the Commissioner of Internal Revenue and under the supervision of the Secretary of the Treasury. Every individual with a gross income of $600 or more and every corporation is required to file an income tax return. Current collection of tax during the year the income is obtained is accomplished by the withholding of individual income tax on wages and salaries and the periodic payment by some individual and corporate taxpayers of an estimated tax on other forms of income. Most disputes involving claimed deficiencies in the payment of taxes or claimed refunds for overpayment are settled informally at the administrative level. Taxpayers' appeals from deficiencies asserted by the Commissioner are heard by the Tax Court of the United States, an independent agency in the executive branch of government which functions much like a true court. In the alternative, the taxpayer may pay the asserted deficiency and sue for a refund in a federal district court or the United States Court of Claims, which have jurisdiction over refund suits.[39] Nonpayment of income tax may also be punishable by civil penalties, collected along with the deficiency, and in some cases by criminal sanctions imposed in a separate proceeding.

The federal income tax, both individual and corporate, is essentially non-schedular, that is the rates are the same for all kinds of income. There are, however, a few kinds of income which are wholly or partly tax exempt. Moreover, gains and losses from the sale of capital assets, such as real property or shares of stock, are treated differently from income, and long term capital gains are taxed at a lower rate, both as to individuals and corporations.[40] The favorable treatment of capital gains is particularly significant because of the broad definition of capital assets. Income tax rates for individuals increase progressively to a maxi-

---

[39] Appeals from the Tax Court and the district courts are heard by the federal courts of appeals, and may go to the Supreme Court on certiorari. Review of cases in the Court of Claims is only by the Supreme Court on certiorari.

[40] The top rate on long term capital gains, that is gains where ownership of the capital asset was for more than six months, is 25%.

mum of 87% of taxable income;[41] the rate for corporations is 52%.[42] The individual income tax is distinguished by the wide variety of deductions which are allowed, including, for example, charitable contributions, expenses in the production of income, exceptional medical expenses, and state and local taxes. These deductions, together with exemptions, result in a very significant lessening of the amount of taxable income to which the rates apply.[43] The intricacy of the subject matter together with the high rates of income taxation have contributed to the rise of a specialized segment of the bar which advises chiefly on tax matters, and the law of federal income taxation is now studied in a separate course in law school by the overwhelming majority of students.

SUGGESTED READINGS

One-volume introductions include Stanley and Kilcullen, *The Federal Income Tax* (4th ed. 1961), and *Montgomery's Federal Taxes*, which is usually revised annually. A brief and elementary survey of both the law and administration of federal taxation is contained in Crockett, *The Federal Tax System of the United States* (1955). Mertens, *The Law of Federal Income Taxation* (rev. ed. by Zimet) is a treatise on the federal income tax in approximately twenty loose-leaf volumes. Mertens, *The Law of Federal Gift and Estate Taxation* (1959-60) is a treatise on federal estate and gift tax in six volumes with current pocket supplements, and Lowndes and Kramer, *Federal Estate and Gift Taxes* (2nd ed. 1962) is a one-volume work on the same subject.

---

41 The tax is payable on net taxable income, after exemptions and deductions have been taken into account. Thus a man with an income of $6,000 and a wife and two children would have exemptions of $600 each for himself and his three dependents, plus a standard deduction of 10% of his gross income if he did not choose to itemize his deductions. He would thus be taxed on only $3,000.

42 This is the rate on income in excess of $25,000. The rate on the first $25,000 is 30%.

43 It has been calculated that in 1954, "for individuals in the income classes $100,000 and above the average rate of tax for the entire group was 48.1 per cent, based on a comparison of adjusted gross income and tax paid. If we add to adjusted gross income an estimate for certain items not included in that figure (tax-exempt interest and one-half of capital gains), the average rate becomes 37.5 per cent. . . . Yet the effective rate in the tax table in section 1 of the law at $100,000 is 67.3 per cent, at $200,000 it is 78.4 per cent, at $500,000 it is 86 per cent, and the maximum is 87 per cent." Surrey, *The Federal Income Tax Base for Individuals*, 58 Colum. L. Rev. 815, 816 (1958).

Bittker, *Federal Income Taxation of Corporations and Share-holders* (1959) is a volume on one important aspect of the income tax laws. Two useful series of pamphlets are published by the Practising Law Institute under the titles *Fundamentals of Federal Taxation* and *Current Problems in Federal Taxation.* Texts on the economic aspects of taxation include Shultz and Harriss, *American Public Finance* (7th ed. 1959), and Blough, *The Federal Taxing Process* (1952). *A 1954 Draft Federal Income Tax Statute,* with comments, was prepared by the American Law Institute and can be compared with the 1954 Code.

CRIMINAL LAW

Scope and Sources

Although American criminal law was derived from that of England at a time when it was largely case law, its basis is now chiefly statutory. Each state has its own penal statutes, and the federal government, while it has no general authority to legislate in this field, has enacted penal statutes under its commerce, taxing, and postal powers.[44] In the federal and some state courts no wrong is punishable as a crime unless it has been made so by statute; in other states the so-called "common law crimes," those traditionally defined by case law, are punishable even if not mentioned by statute. But the difference is not great in practice, for penal statutes in most states are so unsystematic that even if all crimes are mentioned, case law must often be consulted for definitions and general principles. Only a few states have true codes dealing with all major problems of criminal law, and in most jurisdictions criminal law has suffered from years of neglect. To help remedy the situation, the American Law Institute sponsored a Model Penal Code, which was approved in 1962 after a decade of work. Although it is not expected to unify completely the criminal law, it represents a fundamental reconsideration of the subject and had begun to influence federal and state law even before its completion.

---

[44] The great majority of convictions are by the state courts. In 1959 federal penal institutions received just under 14,000 prisoners from the federal courts, while state institutions received nearly 74,000 from the state courts. Sellin, *Crime and Delinquency in the United States: An Over-All View,* 339 The Annals of the American Academy of Political and Social Science 11, 12 (1962). Criminal justice in the armed forces of the United States is subject to the Uniform Code of Military Justice, effective in 1951, which created the Court of Military Appeals, a bench of three civilian judges, to review courts-martial.

CHARACTERISTICS

Three important groups of problems in criminal law involve the definition and classification of offenses, the determination and imposition of punishment, and the basis of criminal responsibility and of exculpation. Definition and classification has suffered in the United States from the absence of any consistent framework such as might have been provided by codification. Although the major crimes are in broad outline largely the same as in other legal systems, particular offenses are often overlapping and highly specific and are characteristically the products of piecemeal development by both case law and legislation. The law of theft, for example, is noted for its technical and irrational distinctions. Crimes are commonly divided into two major categories, felonies and misdemeanors. Felonies traditionally included such serious offenses as murder, manslaughter, arson, rape, robbery, burglary, and larceny; lesser offenses were known as misdemeanors. Today the dividing line between felonies and misdemeanors is usually drawn in terms of either the length of the sentence which may be imposed or the type of institution in which imprisonment is authorized. Each crime, such as murder or arson, may also be subdivided into degrees indicating relative seriousness. In addition there are petty offenses, such as traffic violations, which are usually punishable by fine and which are not properly crimes. Schemes of classification show marks of haphazard growth of the law, vary greatly from one jurisdiction to another, and often lack consistency even within a single jurisdiction. The Model Penal Code accomplishes a substantial simplification by dividing offenses into three degrees of felonies, two degrees of misdemeanors, and violations.

One of the major problems in determination and imposition of punishment has been that of disparity in sentencing. Ordinarily the sentence is fixed, within broad statutory limits, by the judge, or occasionally the jury. In only a few states is there appellate review of the sentence, and there is in most jurisdictions no adequate means of assuring equivalent punishment for similar offenses committed under comparable circumstances. There is, however, a tendency to transfer authority over the ultimate execution of the sentence to an independent board of rehabilitation experts. Another major problem concerns the death penalty which, in spite of considerable effort for repeal, has been abolished in only a small minority of states. In the remaining states it may be imposed for murder, and occasionally for a few other serious felonies. Nevertheless, the actual number of executions is both small and declining,[45] and several devices are used to reduce its impact. Thus murder is ordinarily divided into degrees, commonly first and second; the death penalty is reserved for murder in the first degree; and determination of degree is a matter for the jury. Furthermore, the death penalty in capital cases is almost universally discretionary rather than mandatory and the decision is usually left to the jury during its deliberations as to guilt. Although the Model Penal Code takes no position on the abolition of capital punishment, it provides for a separate proceeding to determine whether the death punishment should be imposed in any capital case.

The most intractable of the third group of problems, dealing with the basis of criminal responsibility and of exculpation, relates to the defense of mental defect or disability, popularly known as "insanity." It is everywhere accepted that a person is not criminally responsible for acts committed while he is "insane," but sharp differences have arisen over the legal tests of insanity. The problem is complicated by the fact that the defense is determined by jurors, laymen whose competence to deal with the kind of expert testimony involved is questionable. Many of the states adhere to the traditional *M'Naghten* rule, laid down by an English court over a century ago,[46] under which the jury is instructed to determine whether the defendant had the capacity to know what he was doing and to know that it was wrong. Others have extended the defense to cover cases where the act was the product of an "impulse" made "irresistible" by mental disease. A few have the *Durham* rule,[47] in which the jury is asked only whether the act was "the product of mental disease or defect." The Model Penal Code has adopted yet another test based on whether the accused, "as a result of mental disease or defect [lacked] substantial capacity to appreciate the criminality of his conduct or to conform his conduct to the requirements of law.[48] Its proponents contend that it will avoid both the un-

---

[45] In the entire United States the number of executions for murder was 144 in 1939, 107 in 1949, and 41 in 1959. Collings, *Offenses of Violence Against the Person*, 339 The Annals of the American Academy of Political and Social Science 42, 47 (1962).

[46] *M'Naghten's Case*, 10 Clark & F. 200, 8 Eng. Rep. 718 (1843).

[47] *Durham* v. *United States*, 214 F. 2d 862 (D.C. Cir. 1954).

[48] Model Penal Code §4.01.

certainty of the *Durham* rule, which depends upon the ambiguous word "product," and the narrowness of the *M'Naghten* rule, which is limited to the accused's knowledge without consideration of his self-control.

SUGGESTED READINGS

Three introductory texts are Perkins, *Criminal Law* (1957); Hall, *General Principles of Criminal Law* (2nd ed. 1960); and Clark and Marshall, *A Treatise on the Law of Crimes* (6th ed. by Wingersky 1958). A series of essays on American criminal law designed for European readers has been published in *The Annals of the American Academy of Political and Social Science* for January, 1962 (vol. 339). The *Model Penal Code*, itself, with its extensive comments, is of course a useful source.

Appendix

Case Law

The opinion below shows some of the techniques which may be used by a court faced with an embarassing precedent. New York Personal Property Law §96(1)(2), a part of the Uniform Sales Act, provides that under the circumstances of this case the seller makes an implied warranty that the goods are both merchantable and fit for their intended purpose. A warranty is an absolute engagement and does not require a showing of negligence on the part of the seller, which would obviously have been impossible here. The statute is silent on the question of to whom the warranty is made, but in the leading case of Chysky v. Drake, cited by the court, the New York Court of Appeals held in 1923 that no implied warranty was made to one with whom the seller had no contractual relations, that is, who was not in "privity" of contract with the seller. In succeeding years the harshness of the result was mollified in family situations where one member of the family purchased goods which injured another, by the use of the fiction that the first was acting as agent for the second so that the second, as principal, was in privity with the seller. Until Greenberg v. Lorenz, however, the New York courts had refused to extend the fiction to find that a parent could act as the agent for his child. The report of the case is reprinted from the official reports in its entirety, with the exception of the headnote and the summary of the arguments of the parties.

GREENBERG v. LORENZ

Court of Appeals of New York, 1961.
9 N.Y. 2d 195, 173 N.E. 2d 773.

Appeal, by permission of the Appellate Division of the Supreme Court in the First Judicial Department, from a judgment, entered April 8, 1959, upon an order of said court which modified, on the law, and, as modified, affirmed a determination of the Appellate Term of the Supreme Court in said department (opinion 12 Misc. 2d 883), affirming a judgement of the City Court of the City of New York (Julius J. Gans, J.; opinion 14 Misc. 2d 279), in favor of plaintiffs. By the modification the Appellate Division reversed so much of the determination as affirmed the judgment of the City Court in favor of the infant plaintiff and directed that the complaint of the infant plaintiff be dismissed.

Chief Judge DESMOND. The infant plaintiff and her father sue a retail food dealer for damages for breach of alleged warranties of fitness and wholesomeness (Personal Property Law, §96, subds. 1, 2). Defendant, they say, sold the father a can of salmon for consumption in the family home. The tinned fish, so it is alleged, was unfit for use as food because it contained some pieces of sharp metal which injured the child's teeth and mouth. The trial at City Court produced a judgment for both plaintiffs on the warranty theory. The Trial Justice commented on the trend away from such decisions as Chysky v. Drake Bros. Co. (235 N. Y. 468) and Redmond v. Borden's Farm Prods. Co. (245 N. Y. 512) and held that although the father had bought the can of salmon the implied warranty extended to his 15-year-old daughter as a member of his household. The Appellate Term affirmed by a vote of 2 to 1. The majority in that court held that the old cases were no longer controlling. The Appellate Division, however, decided (nonunanimously) that the Chysky case is still law and that it forbids a recovery on warranty breach to anyone except the purchaser. As the case comes to us, the father has a judgment for his expenses but the child's own suit has been dismissed for lack of privity.

Our difficulty is not in finding the applicable rule but in deciding whether or not to change it. The decisions are clear enough. There can be no warranty, express or implied, without privity of contract (Turner v. Edison Stor. Battery Co., 248 N. Y. 73, 74; Pearlman v. Garrod Shoe Co., 276 N. Y. 172) since a warranty is an incident of a contract of sale (Fairbank Canning Co. v. Metzger, 118 N. Y. 260, 265). The warranty does not run with the chattel (Nichols v. Clark, MacMullen & Riley, 261 N. Y. 118). Therefore, as to food or other merchandise, there are no implied warranties of merchantability or fitness except as to the buyer (Chysky v. Drake Bros. Co., 235 N. Y. 468, *supra;* Ryan v. Progressive Grocery Stores, 255 N. Y. 388). A wife buying food for her husband may be considered his agent so as to allow a recovery by him (Ryan v. Progressive Grocery Stores, *supra*) and she can bring an action of her own if she makes the purchase and suffers from the breach of warranty (Gimenez v. Great A. & P. Tea Co., 264 N. Y. 390). When two sisters lived in a common household, the one who bought the food was deemed an agent of the other (Bowman v. Great A. & P. Tea Co., 308 N. Y. 780). The same (Bowman) theory was expanded to let both husband and wife recover (Mouren v. Great A. & P. Tea Co., 1 N. Y. 2d 884). But a dependent child is not a contracting party and cannot be a warrantee so no damages are due him (Redmond v. Borden's Farm Prods. Co., 245 N. Y. 512, *supra*).

The unfairness of the restriction has been argued in writings so numerous as to make a lengthy bibliography (see, as examples: Starke, Implied Warranties of Quality and Wholesomeness in the Sale of Food, N.Y.L.J., April 8, 9, 10, 1957, p. 4, col. 1 [Vol. 137, Nos. 67-69]; 1943 Report of N. Y. Law Rev. Comm., p. 413; 1945 Report of N. Y. Law Rev. Comm., p. 23; 1959 Report of N. Y. Law Rev. Comm., p. 57; Miller, N. Y. State Bar Bulletin, Oct., 1952, p. 313; Melick, Sale of Food and Drink, p. 94; Prosser, Torts [2d ed.], p. 493; 29 Fordham L. Rev. 183 [Oct., 1960]; 44 Cornell L. Q. 608; 34 N.Y.U.L. Rev. 1442; 35 St. John's L. Rev. 178 [Dec., 1960]). About 20 States have abolished such requirements of privity, the latest being Virginia and New Jersey (Swift & Co. v. Wells, 201 Va. 213 [1959]; Henningsen v. Bloomfield Motors, 32 N. J. 358 [1960]). The Uniform Commercial Code (§2-318) provides that: "A seller's warranty whether express or implied extends to any natural person who is in the family or household of his buyer or who is a guest in his home if it is reasonable to expect that such person may use, consume or be affected by the goods and who is injured in person by breach of the warranty." [1] In 1943, 1945 and 1959 the New York State Law Revision Commission, each time after careful study, recommended that the implied warranty of fitness for use should extend to the buyers household, members, employees and guests. The Legislature did not act on any of the commission's proposals.

The injustice of denying damages to a child because of non-privity seems too plain for argument. The only real doubt is as to the propriety of changing the rule. Of course, objection will be made (as it has been made before in other such situations, see Woods v. Lancet, 303 N. Y. 349; Bing v. Thunig, 2 N. Y. 2d 656). But the present rule which we are being asked to modify is itself of judicial making since our statutes say nothing at all about privity and in early times such liabilities were thought to be in tort (Prosser, Torts [2d ed.], p. 507; 1 Williston on Sales [Rev. ed.], p. 502). Alteration of the law in such matters has been the business of the New York courts for many years (MacPherson v. Buick Motor Co., 217 N. Y. 382; Ultramares Corp. v. Touche, 255 N. Y. 170).

The Ryan, Gimenez and Bowman cases (*supra*) in our court show an increasing tendency to lessen the rigors of the rule. In Blessington v. McCrory Stores Corp. (305 N. Y. 140) we passed on a Statute of Limitations point only but we did not (as we could have under the old cases) dismiss for insufficiency a complaint which demanded damages for an infant's death when the dangerous article had been purchased by the infant's mother. There are a great many well-considered lower court decisions in this State which attest to the prevalent feeling that at least as to injured members of a buyer's family the strict privity rule is unfair and should be revised.

So convincing a showing of injustice and impracticality calls upon us to move but we should be cautious and take one step at a time. To decide the case before us, we should hold that the infant's cause of action should not have been dismissed solely on the ground that the food was purchased not by the child but by the child's father. Today when so much of our food is bought in packages it is not just or sensible to confine the warranty's protection to the individual buyer. At least as to food and household goods, the presumption should be that the purchase was made for all the members of the household.

Sections 199-a and 200 of the Agriculture and Markets Law have no relevance here since those laws refer to food which has become unfit because of adulteration, decomposition, etc.

The judgment should be modified by reinstating the infant's recovery and, as so modified, affirmed, with costs to the plaintiffs in this court and in the Appellate Division.

FROESSEL, J. (concurring). I concur for modification here, but limited to the facts of this case. The infant plaintiff asked for the food purchased, and it was but normal that the father, who was in any event liable for her necessaries, should make the purchase on behalf of both (see Bowman v. Great A. & P. Tea Co., 308 N. Y. 780).

---

[1] The Uniform Commercial Code was adopted in New York in 1962, effective in 1964.

The Chief Judge has clearly and succinctly stated the problem before us, and has reviewed the applicable authorities. This is an action in contract based on a statute (Personal Property Law, §96), not for negligence, and it is basic law that unless privity exists there can be no warranty, and where there is no warranty there can be no breach. We may not convert an action in contract into what really amounts to an action in tort.

However much one may think liability should be broadened, that must be left to the Legislature. There are two sides to the problem before us— and one of them is the plight of the seller. It is just as unfair to hold liable a retail groceryman, as here, who is innocent of any negligence or wrong, on the theory of breach of warranty, for some defect in a canned product which he could not inspect and with the production of which he had nothing to do, as it is to deny relief to one who has no relationship to the contract of purchase and sale, though eating at the purchaser's table. As Justice Steuer aptly observed at the Appellate Term, "it may be odd that the purchaser can recover while others cannot, but it is odder still that one without fault has to pay at all." This distinguishes these cases from situations such as presented in Woods v. Lancet (303 N. Y. 349) and Bing v. Thunig (2 N. Y. 2d 656), where the defendant has clearly committed a wrong.

It is for the Legislature to determine the policy of accommodating those conflicting interests after affording all concerned an opportunity to be heard. Indeed, the Legislature has not been unaware of the problem for, in three separate years—1943, 1945, 1959—as noted by the Chief Judge, the New York State Law Revision Commission recommended that the benefits of implied warranties be extended to the buyer's employees and to the members of his household, but the Legislature has declined to act, despite the introduction of legislation. I do not think we should now assume their powers and change the rules, which will undoubtedly affect many cases in which lawyers and litigants understood the law to be otherwise, and governed themselves accordingly.

Judges Dye, Fuld, Van Voorhis, Burke and Foster concur with Chief Judge Desmond; Judge Froessel concurs in result in a separate opinion.

Judgment accordingly.

Statutes

The following opinion well illustrates a variety of techniques of statutory interpretation. It concerns the Safety Appliance Act of March 2, 1893, one of the early industrial safety acts that preceded workmen's compensation legislation. The act, which as amended is found today in sections 1-7 of Title 45 of the United States Code, suggests the detail common to much American legislation. Workmen seeking to recover from their employers under case law for injuries sustained during their employment had been met not only by the defense of contributory negligence, but also by the defense of assumption of risk. This latter defense was developed by the courts on the premise that the employee, conscious of the hazards of his employment, had impliedly agreed to assume the risk of injury which resulted from them when he entered upon his employment. In this case the injured workman relied on the Safety Appliance Act in order to avoid the defense. The statute in its entirety, as enacted in 1893, is set out below, followed by the opinion of the Court. The headnote and the arguments of the parties have been omitted.

An act to promote the safety of employees and travelers upon railroads by compelling common carriers engaged in interstate commerce to equip their cars with automatic couplers and continuous brakes and their locomotives with driving-wheel brakes, and for other purposes.

Be it enacted by the Senate and House of Representatives of the United states of America in Congress assembled, That from and after the first day of January, eighteen hundred and ninety-eight, it shall be unlawful for any common carrier engaged in interstate commerce by railroad to use on its line any locomotive engine in moving interstate traffic not equipped with a power driving-wheel brake and appliances for operating the train-brake system, or to run any train in such traffic after said date that has not a sufficient number of cars in it so equipped with power or train brakes that the engineer on the locomotive drawing such train can control its speed without requiring brakemen to use the common hand brake for that purpose.

SEC. 2.   That on and after the first day of January, eighteen hundred and ninety-eight, it shall be unlawful for any such common carrier to haul or permit to be hauled or used on its line any car used in moving interstate traffic not equipped with couplers coupling automatically by impact, and which can be uncoupled without the necessity of men going between the ends of the cars.

SEC. 3.   That when any person, firm, company, or corporation engaged in interstate commerce by railroad shall have equipped a sufficient number of its cars so as to comply with the provisions of section one of this act, it may lawfully refuse to receive from connecting lines of road or shippers any car not equipped sufficiently, in accordance with the first section of this act, with such power or train brakes as will work and readily interchange with the brakes in use on its own cars, as required by this act.

SEC. 4.   That from and after the first day of July, eighteen hundred and ninety-five, until otherwise ordered by the Interstate Commerce Commission, it shall be unlawful for any railroad company to use any car in interstate commerce that is not provided with secure grab irons or handholds in the ends and sides of each car for greater security to men in coupling and uncoupling cars.

SEC. 5.   That within ninety days from the passage of this act the American Railway Association is authorized hereby to designate to the Interstate Commerce Commission the standard height of drawbars for freight cars, measured perpendicular from the level of the tops of the rails to the centers of the drawbars, for each of the several gauges of railroads in use in the United States, and shall fix a maximum variation from such standard height to be allowed between the drawbars of empty and loaded cars. Upon their determination being certified to the Interstate Commerce Commission, said Commission shall at once give notice of the standard fixed upon to all common carriers, owners, or leasees engaged in interstate commerce in the United States by such means as the Commission may deem proper. But should said association fail to determine a standard as above provided, it shall be the duty of the Interstate Commerce Commission to do so, before July first, eighteen hundred and ninety-four, and immediately to give notice thereof as aforesaid. And after July first, eighteen hundred and ninety-five, no cars, either loaded or unloaded, shall be used in interstate traffic which do not comply with the standard above provided for.

Sec. 6. That any such common carrier using any locomotive engine, running any train, or hauling or permitting to be hauled or used on its line any car in violation of any of the provisions of this act, shall be liable to a penalty of one hundred dollars for each and every violation, to be recovered in a suit or suits to be brought by the United States district attorney in the district court of the United States having jurisdiction in the locality where such violation shall have been committed, and it shall be the duty of such district attorney to bring such suits upon duly verified information being lodged with him of such violation having occured. And it shall also be the duty of the Interstate Commerce Commission to lodge with the proper district attorneys information of any such violations as may come to its knowledge: *Provided*, That nothing in this act contained shall apply to trains composed of four-wheel cars or to locomotives used in hauling such trains.

Sec. 7. That the Interstate Commerce Commission may from time to time upon full hearing and for good cause extend the period within which any common carrier shall comply with the provisions of this act.

Sec. 8. That any employee of any such common carrier who may be injured by any locomotive, car, or train in use contrary to the provision of this act shall not be deemed thereby to have assumed the risk thereby occasioned, although continuing in the employment of such carrier after the unlawful use of such locomotive, car, or train had been brought to his knowledge.

Approved, March 2, 1893.

JOHNSON v. SOUTHERN PACIFIC CO.

Supreme Court of the United States, 1904.
196 U. S. 1, 25 S. Ct. 158, 49 L. Ed. 363.

Johnson brought this action in the District Court of the First Judicial District of Utah against the Southern Pacific Company to recover damages for injuries received while employed by that company as a brakeman. The case was removed to the Circuit Court of the United States for the District of Utah by defendant on the ground of diversity of citizenship.

The facts were briefly these: August 5, 1900, Johnson was acting as head brakeman on a freight train of the Southern Pacific Company, which was making its regular trip between San Francisco, California, and Ogden, Utah. On reaching the town of Promontory, Utah, Johnson was directed to uncouple the engine from the train and couple it to a dining car, belonging to the company, which was standing on a side track, for the purpose of turning the car around preparatory to its being picked up and put on the next west-bound passenger train. The engine and the dining car were equipped, respectively, with the Janney coupler and the Miller hook, so called, which would not couple together automatically by impact, and it was, therefore, necessary for Johnson, and he was ordered, to go between the engine and the dining car, to accomplish the coupling. In so doing Johnson's hand was caught between the engine bumper and the dining car bumper and crushed, which necessitated amputation of the hand above the wrist.

On the trial of the case, defendant, after plaintiff had rested, moved the court to instruct the jury to find in its favor, which motion was granted, and the jury found a verdict accordingly, on which judgment was entered. Plaintiff carried the case to the Circuit Court of Appeals for the Eighth Circuit and the judgment was affirmed. 117 Fed. Rep. 462.

MR. CHIEF JUSTICE FULLER, after making the foregoing statement, delivered the opinion of the court.

This case was brought here on certiorari, and also on writ of error, and will be determined on the merits, without discussing the question of jurisdiction as between the one writ and the other. Pullman's Car Company v. Transportation Company, 171 U. S. 138, 145.

The plaintiff claimed that he was relieved of assumption of risk under common law rules by the act of Congress of March 2, 1893, 27 Stat. 531, c. 196, entitled "An act to promote the safety of employees and travelers upon railroads by compelling common carriers engaged in interstate commerce to equip their cars with automatic couplers and continuous brakes and their locomotives with driving-wheel brakes, and for other purposes."

The issues involved questions deemed of such general importance that the Government was permitted to file brief and be heard at the bar.

The act of 1893 provided: [Here the Court quoted from sections 1, 2, 6, and 8 of the act.]

The Circuit Court of Appeals held, in substance, Sanborn, J., delivering the opinion and Lochren, J., concurring, that the locomotive and car were both equipped as required by the act, as the one had a power driving-wheel brake and the other a coupler; that section 2 did not apply to locomotives; that at the time of the accident the dining car was not "used in moving interestate traffic;" and, moreover, that the locomotive, as well as the dining car, was furnished with an automatic coupler so that each was equipped as the statute required if section 2 applied to both. Thayer, J., concurred in the judgment on the latter ground, but was of opinion that locomotives were included by the words "any car" in the second section, and that the dining car was being "used in moving interstate traffic."

We are unable to accept these conclusions, notwithstanding the able opinion of the majority, as they appear to us to be inconsistent with the plain intention of Congress, to defeat the object of the legislation, and to be arrived at by an inadmissible narrowness of construction.

The intention of Congress, declared in the preamble and in sections one and two of the act, was "to promote the safety of employees and travelers upon railroads by compelling common carriers engaged in interstate commerce to equip their cars with automatic couplers and continuous brakes and their locomotives with driving-wheel brakes," those brakes to be accompanied with "appliances for operating the train-brake system;" and every car to be "equipped with couplers coupling automatically by impact, and which can be uncoupled without the necessity of men going between the ends of the cars," whereby the danger and risk consequent on the existing system was averted as far as possible.

The present case is that of an injured employee, and involves the application of the act in respect of automatic couplers, the preliminary question being whether locomotives are required to be equipped with such couplers. And it is not to be successfully denied that they are so required if the words "any car" of the second section were intended to embrace, and do embrace, locomotives. But it is said that this cannot be so because locomotives were elsewhere in terms required to be equipped with power driving-wheel brakes, and that the rule that the expression of one thing excludes another applies. That, however, is a question of intention, and as there was special reason for requiring locomotives to be equipped with power driving-wheel brakes, if it were also necessary that locomotives should be equipped with automatic couplers, and the word "car" would cover locomotives, then the intention to limit the equipment of locomotives to power driving-wheel brakes, because they were separately mentioned, could not be imputed. Now it was as necessary for the safety of employees in coupling and uncoupling, that locomotives should be equipped with automatic couplers, as it was that freight and passenger and dining cars should be, perhaps more so, as Judge Thayer suggests, "since engines have occasion to make couplings more frequently."

And manifestly the word "car" was used in its generic sense. There is nothing to indicate that any particular kind of car was meant. Tested by context, subject matter and object, "any car" meant all kinds of cars running on the rails, including locomotives. And this view is supported by the dictionary definitions and by many judicial decisions, some of them having been rendered in construction of this act. Winkler v. Philadelphia & Reading Railway Company, 53 Atl. Rep. 90; 4 Penn. (Del.) 387; Fleming v. Southern Railway Company, 131 N. Car. 476; East St. Louis Connecting Railway Company v. O'Hara, 150 Illinois, 580; Kansas City &c. Railroad Company v. Crocker, 95 Alabama, 412; Thomas v. Georgia Railroad and Banking Company, 38 Georgia, 222; Mayor &c. v. Third Ave. R. R. Co., 117 N. Y. 404; Benson v. Railway Company, 75 Minnesota, 163.

The result is that if the locomotive in question was not equipped with automatic couplers, the company failed to comply with the provisions of the act. It appears, however, that this locomotive was in fact equipped with automatic couplers, as well as the dining car, but that the couplers on each, which were of different types, would not couple with each other automatically by impact so as to render it unnecessary for men to go between the cars to couple and uncouple.

Nevertheless, the Circuit Court of Appeals was of opinion that it would be an unwarrantable extension of the terms of the law to hold that where the couplers would couple automatically with couplers of their own kind, the couplers must so couple with couplers of different kinds. But we think that what the act plainly forbade was the use of cars which could not be coupled together automatically by impact, by means of the couplers actually used on the cars to be coupled. The object was to protect the lives and limbs of railroad employees by rendering it unnecessary for a man operating the couplers to go between the ends of the cars, and that object would be defeated, not necessarily by the use of automatic couplers of different kinds, but if those different kinds would not automatically couple with each other. The point was that the railroad companies should be compelled, respectively, to adopt devices, whatever they were, which would act so far uniformly as to eliminate the danger consequent on men going between the cars.

If the language used were open to construction, we are constrained to say that the construction put upon the act by the Circuit Court of Appeals was altogether too narrow.

This strictness was thought to be required because the common law rule as to the assumption of risk was changed by the act, and because the act was penal.

The dogma as to the strict construction of statutes in deregation of the common law only amounts to the recognition of a presumption against an intention to change existing law, and as there is no doubt of that intention here, the extent of the application of the change demands at least no more rigorous construction than would be applied to penal laws. And, as Chief Justice Parker remarked, conceding that statutes in derogation of the common law are to be construed strictly, "they are also to be construed sensibly, and with a view to the object aimed at by the legislature." Gibson v. Jenney, 15 Massachusetts, 205.

The primary object of the act was to promote the public welfare by securing the safety of employees and travelers, and it was in that aspect remedial, while for violations a penalty of one hundred dollars, recoverable in a civil action, was provided for, and in that aspect it was penal. But the design to give relief was more dominant than to inflict punishment, and the act might well be held to fall within the rule applicable to statutes to prevent fraud upon the revenue, and for the collection of customs, that rule not requiring absolute strictness of construction. Taylor v. United States, 3 How. 197; United States v. Stowell, 133 U.S. 1, 12, and cases cited. And see Farmers' and Merchants' National Bank v. Dearing, 91 U. S. 29, 35; Gray v. Bennett, 3 Met. (Mass.) 522.

Moreover, it is settled that "though penal laws are to be construed strictly, yet the intention of the legislation must govern in the construction of penal as well as oher statutes; and they are not to be construed so strictly as to defeat the obvious intention of the legislature." United States v. Lacher, 134 U. S. 624. In that case we cited and quoted from United States v. Winn, 3 Sumn. 209, in which Mr. Justice Story, referring to the rule that penal statutes are to be construed strictly, said:

"I agree to that rule in its true and sober sense; and that is, that penal statutes are not to be enlarged by implication, or extended to cases not obviously within their words and purport. But where the words are general, and include various classes of persons, I know of no authority, which would justify the court in restricting them to one class, or in giving them the narrowest interpretation, where the mischief to be redressed by the statute is equally applicable to all of them. And where a word is used in a statute, which has various known significations, I know of no rule, that requires the court to adopt one in preference to another, simply because it is more restrained, if the objects of the statute equally apply to the largest and broadest sense of the word. In short, it appears to me, that the proper course in all these cases, is to search out and follow the true intent of the legislature, and to adopt that sense of the words which harmonizes best with the context, and promotes in the fullest manner, the apparent policy and objects of the legislature."

Tested by these principles, we think the view of the Circuit Court of Appeals, which limits the second section to merely providing automatic couplers, does not give due effect to the words "coupling automatically by impact, and which can be uncoupled without the necessity of men going between the cars," and cannot be sustained.

We dismiss as without merit the suggestion, which has been made, that the words "without the necessity of men going between the ends of the cars," which are the test of compliance with section two, apply only to the act of uncoupling. The phrase literally covers both coupling and un-coupling, and if read, as it should be, with a comma after the word "un-coupled," this becomes entirely clear. Chicago, Milwaukee & St. Paul Railway Company v. Voelker, 129 Fed. Rep. 522; United States v. Lacher, *supra*.

The risk in coupling and uncoupling was the evil sought to be rem-edied, and that risk was to be obviated by the use of couplers actually coupling automatically. True, no particular design was required, but what-ever the devices used they were to be effectively interchangeable. Con-gress was not paltering in a double sense. And its intention is found "in the language actually used, interpreted according to its fair and obvious mean-ing." United States v. Harris, 177 U. S. 305, 309.

That this was the scope of the statute is confirmed by the circum-stances surrounding its enactment, as exhibited in public documents to which we are at liberty to refer. Binns v. United States, 194 U. S. 486, 495; Holy Trinity Church v. United States, 143 U. S. 457, 463.

President Harrison, in his annual messages of 1889, 1890, 1891 and 1892, earnestly urged upon Congress the necessity of legislation to obviate and reduce the loss of life and the injuries due to the prevailing method of coupling and braking. In his first message he said: "It is competent, I think, for Congress to require uniformity in the construction of cars used in interstate commerce, and the use of improved safety appliances upon such trains. Time will be necessary to make the needed changes, but an earnest and intelligent beginning should be made at once. It is a reproach to our civilization that any class of American workmen should, in the pur-suit of a necessary and useful vocation, be subjected to a peril of life and limb as great as that of a soldier in time of war."

And he reiterated his recommendation in succeeding messages, saying in that for 1892: "Statistics furnished by the Interstate Commerce Com-mission show that during the year ending June 30, 1891, there were forty-seven different styles of car couplers reported to be in use, and that during the same period there were 2,660 employees killed and 26,140 injured. Nearly 16 per cent of the deaths occurred in the coupling and uncoupling of cars, and over 36 per cent of the injuries had the same origin."

The Senate report of the first session of the Fifty-second Congress (No. 1049), and the House report of the same session (No. 1678), set out the numerous and increasing casualties due to coupling, the demand for protection, and the necessity of automatic couplers, coupling inter-changeably. The difficulties in the case were fully expounded and the result reached to require an automatic coupling by impact so as to render it unnecessary for men to go between the cars, while no particular device or type was adopted, the railroad companies being left free to work out the details for themselves, ample time being given for that purpose. The law gave five years, and that was enlarged, by the Interstate Commerce Commission as authorized by law, two years, and subsequently seven months, making seven years and seven months in all.

The diligence of counsel has called our attention to changes made in the bill in the course of its passage, and to the debates in the Senate on the report of its committee. 24 Cong. Rec., pt. 2, pp. 1246, 1273 *et seq.* These demonstrate that the difficulty as to interchangeability was fully in the mind of Congress and was assumed to be met by the language which was used. The essential degree of uniformity was secured by providing that the couplings must couple automatically by impact without the necessity of men going between the ends of the cars.

In the present case the couplings would not work together, Johnson was obliged to go between the cars, and the law was not complied with.

March 2, 1903, 32 Stat. 943, c. 976, an act in amendment of the act of 1893 was approved, which provided, among other things, that the provisions and requirements of the former act "shall be held to apply to common carriers by railroads in the Territories and the District of Columbia and shall apply in all cases, whether or not the couplers brought together are of the same kind, make, or type;" and "shall be held to apply to all trains, locomotives, tenders, cars, and similar vehicles used on any railroad engaged in interstate commerce."

This act was to take effect September first, nineteen hundred and three, and nothing in it was to be held or construed to relieve any common carrier "from any of the provisions, powers, duties, liabilities, or requirements" of the act of 1893, all of which should apply except as specifically amended.

As we have no doubt of the meaning of the prior law, the subsequent legislation cannot be regarded as intended to operate to destroy it. Indeed, the latter act is affirmative, and declaratory, and, in effect, only construed and applied the former act. Bailey v. Clark, 21 Wall. 284; United States *v.* Freeman, 3 How. 556; Cope v. Cope, 137 U. S. 682; Wetmore v. Markoe, *post,* p. 68. This legislative recognition of the scope of the prior law fortifies and does not weaken the conclusion at which we have arrived.

Another ground on which the decision of the Circuit Court of Appeals was rested remains to be noticed. That court held by a majority that as the dining car was empty and had not actually entered upon its trip, it was not used in moving interstate traffic, and hence was not within the act. The dining car had been constantly used for several years to furnish meals to passengers between San Francisco and Ogden, and for no other purpose. On the day of the accident the eastbound train was so late that it was found that the car could not reach Ogden in time to return on the next westbound train according to intention, and it was therefore dropped off at Promontory to be picked up by that train as it came along that evening.

The presumption is that it was stocked for the return, and as it was not a new car, or a car just from the repair shop, on its way to its field of labor, it was not "an empty," as that term is sometimes used. Besides, whether cars are empty or loaded, the danger to employees is practically the same, and we agree with the observation of District Judge Shiras in Voelker v. Railway Company, 116 Fed. Rep. 867, that "it cannot be true that on the eastern trip the provisions of the act of Congress would be binding upon the company, because the cars were loaded, but would not be binding upon the return trip, because the cars are empty."

Counsel urges that the character of the dining car at the time and place of the injury was local only and could not be changed until the car was actually engaged in interstate movement or being put into a train for such use, and Coe v. Errol, 116 U. S. 517, is cited as supporting that contention. In Coe v. Errol it was held that certain logs cut in New Hampshire, and hauled to a river in order that they might be transported to Maine, were subject to taxation in the former State before transportation had begun.

The distinction between merchandise which may become an article of interstate commerce, or may not, and an instrument regularly used in moving interstate commerce, which has stopped temporarily in making its trip between two points in different States, renders this and like cases inapplicable.

Confessedly this dining car was under the control of Congress while in the act of making its interstate journey, and in our judgment it was equally so when waiting for the train to be made up for the next trip. It was being regularly used in the movement of interstate traffic and so within the law.

Finally it is argued that Johnson was guilty of such contributory negligence as to defeat recovery, and that, therefore, the judgement should be affirmed. But the Circuit Court of Appeals did not consider this question, nor apparently did the Circuit Court, and we do not feel constrained to inquire whether it could have been open under § 8, or if so, whether it should have been left to the jury under proper instructions.

The judgment of the Circuit Court of Appeals is reversed; the judgment of the Circuit Court is also reversed, and the cause remanded to that court with instructions to set aside the verdict and award a new trial.

Index